THE FOUR HUNDRED SILENT YEARS

(From Malachi to Matthew)

Illustrated

H. A. IRONSIDE

Author of "Lectures on Daniel;" "Notes on Ezra, Nehemiah and Esther;" "Notes on the Minor Prophets," etc., etc.

NEW YORK
LOIZEAUX BROTHERS, BIBLE TRUTH DEPOT
1 EAST 13TH STREET

CONTENTS

PREFACE

SOME time ago I endeavored, though with no claim to originality of treatment, to draw practical lessons for the separated people of God from the captivity and post-captivity books of the Old Testament. At the suggestion of the publishers I have now sought to trace the history of the same people through the years of waiting that elapsed from the time when the voice of inspiration ceased until the heavens resounded with the glad announcement of "Glory to God in the highest, and on earth peace, good-will toward men," thus heralding Messiah's long-promised advent.

In preparing this work, I have been greatly helped by a series of papers entitled, "From Malachi to Matthew," which appeared a number of years ago in an English periodical now discontinued.[1] Dr. Grant's "Between the Testaments" has also been consulted, and had that volume been more in accord with a belief in the plenary inspiration of Scripture, the book now in my reader's hand might perhaps not have been prepared. The Old Testament Apocrypha, (especially I. Maccabees), Josephus, and various Jewish histories of recent date, have also afforded considerable help.

It will be observed that my object has been, not merely to give a chronological outline of events, or a series of biographical sketches, but to trace throughout lessons and warnings for any who to-day, as those in the days of Nehemiah, have sought to return to and obey the word of God, in separation from the infidelity and apostasy of the times. Such are exposed to similar dangers—though of a spiritual character—as those

---

[1] *Faithful Words*, edited by H. F. Witherby

which confronted the Jews. From their history we may therefore obtain valuable suggestions, and by carefully considering the causes of their failures, be preserved from falling into the same snares.

History repeats itself in manifold ways, and he who is wise will not despise its instruction. "Happy is the man that feareth alway;" for he who thinks he stands, is the one who is exhorted to take heed lest he fall.

H. A. IRONSIDE

VICTORIA, B.C.,

March, 1914.

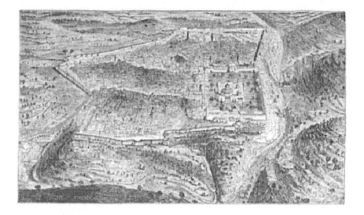

VIEW OF JERUSALEM FROM THE SOUTH.—Jerusalem covers four or five hill-summits. Within the city walls, on the south-east, is Mount Moriah, the site of the temple, now covered by the Haram enclosure or square, within which is the Mosque of Omar. West and south-west of this is Mount Zion, a portion of which is without the city wall. Directly south of Moriah is the hill Ophel, also without the wall. North of Mount Moriah is Bezetha, or the "new city," and west of Bezetha, in the north-west part of the city, is Akra. (Some, however, regard Akra as the north-west art of Mount Zion.). East side of the city is the Kedron, or Valley of Jehoshaphat. South of Mount Zion is the Valley of Hinnom, which extends around on the west side of the city. The valleys of Hinnom and of the Kedron unite south of the city. Between Ophel and Mount Zion is the Tvropœon Valley. North of the city is Scopus, east of it the Mount of Olives, and on the south the Hill of Evil Counsel.

I. THE JEWS UNDER PRIESTLY RULE

(From the times of "Darius the Persian" (Neh. 12:22)
to the fall of the Persian Empire—about 425 to 335,
B.C.)

THE average Bible reader seldom knows much of the stirring events which followed in rapid succession the days of rehabilitation, described in the interesting and instructive records of Ezra and Nehemiah. He gets more than an inkling of the fallen condition of the restored remnant in the solemn expostulation of the last prophet, Malachi; but when he opens the New Testament and begins to read the Gospel of Matthew, he finds an utter change of atmosphere and conditions. The Old Testament closes with the people of the Jews partially restored to their land, but under Persian dominion. The New Testament opens with the same people greatly multiplied and dwelling in the the same country, but under Roman sway, and yet with an Edomite vice-king exercising jurisdiction over part of the land. In many other respects circumstances have undergone a marked change, and generally for the worse.

What brought about these changes? What movements, civil, religious, and political, were in progress during the *four hundred silent years* after prophetic testimony had died away with a last solemn warning of a possible curse to smite the land and people once so richly blessed? (Mal. 4:6).

We cannot turn to the unerring word of God for an authentic and inspired answer to these questions; but we are able, nevertheless, to reply to them with a large measure of assurance, since God has been pleased to preserve, uninspired but fairly reliable, chronicles of the history of His chosen people in the four centuries that succeeded the days of the prophets. The Jewish historian, Josephus, and the unknown (save to God) author of the first book of the Maccabees, have left us records that are generally considered trustworthy, and are largely corroborated by Jewish traditions and historical side-lights.

With Nehemiah, the history and experiences of the returned Remnant in the Land end, at a time when evil was creeping in and decay was beginning. In his lifetime Nehemiah earnestly endeavored to uphold their covenant-relation with God, and zealously sought to maintain that holy separation from the idolatrous nations surrounding them, as a peculiar people to Jehovah, wherein alone their strength lay. Balaam had declared, "The people shall dwell alone; they shall not be reckoned among the nations," and he had also taught Balak to cast a stumblingblock before Israel by breaking down this very separation. "The doctrine of Balaam" had been their snare ever afterwards, and we see in the closing chapters of Nehemiah how difficult it was to stamp it out.

Nehemiah's efforts were largely successful; and while his godly life and testimony still had influence over the people there was a measure at least of outward separation. But Malachi is witness that people may be separated *from* outside evils and not be separated *to* the Lord. This is a constant danger. Who has not heard "heady, high-minded" believers prating of "separation from evil as God's principle of unity" (as indeed it is, other things being equal), who seem quite to forget that it is separation *to Christ* that alone gives power to the former.

Separation *from*, may end in mere Pharisaism. Separation *to*, will result in practical godliness, and be evidenced by devotedness, with brotherly love and unity.

But this truth ever needs consecrated men of God to insist upon its recognition; otherwise, there is always the likelihood of its being forgotten, and a *form* of godliness without the power usurping its place. Of Israel of old, when first settled in the land, we read: "And Israel served the Lord all the days of Joshua, and all the days of the elders that outlived Joshua, and which had known all the works of the Lord, that He had done for Israel" (Josh. 24:31). We have something analogous to this in the case now under consideration. The Jewish remnant, generally speaking, walked before God in a measure of holy separation and cleaving to His name and His word during the days of Ezra and Nehemiah, and of the elders who outlived them; but even in Malachi's time declension had made very rapid progress.

After the death of Nehemiah the "Tirshatha," or Governor, they enjoyed a large measure of independence under the mild rule of the Persian kings, and even for a time after the Medo-Persian "Bear" had been defeated and superseded by the four-headed "Leopard" of Greece (Dan. 7)—or, using the simile of Nebuchadnezzar's dream, after the silver kingdom had been displaced by the dominion of brass (Dan. 2).

Government was entrusted by these Gentile sovereigns to the high-priest, who previously was but a religious leader. In Nehemiah 12:10, 11, 22,[2] we have

---

[2] "And Jeshua begat Joiakim ; Joiakim also begat Eliashib, and Eliashib begat Joiada; and Joiada begat Jonathan, and Jonathan

the high-priestly line traced down from Jeshua, or Joshua (who came up from Babylon, with Zerubbabel at the first return, and is the one described in Zechariah's vision, chap. 3), through Joiakim, Eliashib, Joiada, and Jonathan to Jaddua, the latest historical character mentioned in the Old Testament.

Eliashib succeeded to the high-priesthood during the life-time of Nehemiah, and it was his grandson (Joiada's son), whom the Tirshatha indignantly "chased" from him because of his unhallowed alliance by marriage with the house of Sanballat the Horonite (Neh. 13:28).

One tradition credits the closing of the canon of Old Testament to the days of Eliashib, before the death of Ezra. "The great synagogue" was supposed to have been presided over by this venerable servant of God (Ezra), and he is generally considered to have largely edited the books and arranged the Psalms in the order in which they are found in the Hebrew Bible. Some have thought to identify him with Malachi, supposing the title "Malachi" to be an untranslated word, simply meaning "My messenger," or "Messenger of Jehovah." But this seems unlikely, as Malachi apparently portrays a later stage of declension. He may have prophesied in the days of Joiada or Jonathan. It is more than likely that another tradition, which gives Simon the Just the credit of settling authoritatively the limits of the canon, is the correct one.

---

begat Jaddua . . . The Levites, in the days of Eliashib, Joiada, and Johanan, and Jaddua, were recorded chief of the fathers: also the priests, to the reign of Darius the Persian "—which was nearly to the end of the Persian Empire.

12

Of these high-priests we know but little, save that Josephus implies that the former (**Joiada**) was exceedingly friendly to the mixed nations surrounding Judea, as indeed seems very likely, from the fact referred to above; his son having wedded the daughter of Sanballat, the arch-conspirator (Nch. 13:28). The Jewish historian, Josephus, declares that this young man, upon being driven out by Nehemiah, went over to the Samaritans, and with the aid of his wealthy and influential father-in-law, established the Samaritan system, and projected the building of a rival temple on Mount Gerizim. Such a temple was in existence as early as the days of Alexander the Great, but whether the unworthy son of Joiada had to do with its building is questionable. It is frequently the case, however, that one outwardly connected with the truth, without knowing its power in the soul, becomes the bitterest enemy of that which is of God, when repudiated for his unholy ways.

Jonathan (who is also called Johanan) left a most unsavory record. He was an insubject, godless man; though he remained to the last among the Jews, even committing the horrid crime of murder to make more secure his own place of authority as high-priest and ruler. He profaned the very temple of God by assassinating his brother Joshua (or Jesus) within its sacred precincts. Thus had corruption and violence so soon found a foothold among the separated remnant, emphasizing the solemn fact that mere correctness of position is of no real value, so far as maintaining what is of God is concerned, unless there be personal piety and devotedness to the Lord. We often hear of being "in the right place," "on the true ground," etc., but they are hollow and empty expressions when divorced from righteousness and holiness of truth. That believers on the Lord Jesus Christ should be a separated, unworldly people, no right-thinking Christian will deny or even question for a moment; but it is to the Holy and the True we are to be set apart, and only as we "go forth unto *Him*," will our separation be of any real value, and we ourselves "vessels unto honor, sanctified and meet for the Master's use."

Man is prone to rest in what is merely outward, while neglecting or coolly ignoring what is inward; for "man looketh on the outward appearance, but God looketh on the heart." Hence the importance of insisting on *reality*, and not being content with mere outward conformity and ecclesiastical order. A Diotrephes will demand the latter while neglecting the former; but, on the other hand, another may be equally wrong if he lays stress only on what is subjective, while paying no attention to to the question of association. The well-balanced Christian will have a care as to both, and neglect neither.

But we must return to our task of tracing out the history of the Jewish people under the high-priestly *regime*, during the years of Persian domination.

Jaddua was exercising the sacerdotal office when, in the course of God's ways, the time had arrived for setting the Persian rule aside and giving it to the Greek. Jaddua was a man of spotless integrity, and his name is held in veneration to the present time.

It is related of him that he was a faithful servant under the kings of Persia; but when Alexander the Great had destroyed Tyre, and driven the armies of Darius Codomanus to the east in confusion, Jaddua was assured that the time had come for the fulfilment of Daniel's prophecy as to the destruction of the second world-empire and its being replaced by the third. He recognized in the youthful Macedonian conqueror the rough he-goat with the notable horn between its eyes, who was to run upon the two-horned ram in the fury of his power and destroy it completely. Hearing that the cities of Syria were falling one by one before him, and that Alexander was actually on his way to besiege Jerusalem, Jaddua is said to have put on his pontifical garments, and with the Scriptures of the Prophets in his hand, to have gone forth to meet the conqueror, attended, not by armed men, but by a body of white-robed priests. As they drew near the army of Alexander, the latter is said to have hastened to meet them, prostrating himself on the ground before Jaddua, declaring he had but recently beheld the venerable pontiff in a vision, and recognized him as the representative of the God of heaven, who would show him what would be greatly to his advantage. Jaddua opened the prophetic roll, and had one of the scribes in his company read the visions of Daniel and their interpretation. Alexander saw the undoubted reference to himself, and declared he would never permit Jerusalem to be touched nor its temple polluted, and sent the high-priest back laden with gifts.

It is impossible at this late day to know whether this story is a mere tradition or sober history; but there is nothing unlikely about it; at least it teaches a valuable lesson, reminding us that the word of God has foretold the end from the beginning, and He who inspired it has declared, "My counsel shall stand, and I will do all My pleasure." Jaddua possessed those Scriptures which reveal God's plans as to the nations of the earth; for prophecy is but history written prior to the events. Therefore it is not at all unreasonable to suppose that he acted as tradition relates.

This is the specific value of the study of prophecy, that it enables one to act in the present in the light of the things that are yet future. So writes the apostle Peter, when he tells us: "We have also the prophetic word made sure; whereunto ye do well that ye take heed in your hearts, as unto a lamp that shineth in a dark place till the day dawn and the day-star arise. Knowing this first, that no prophecy of the Scripture is of its own interpretation; for the prophecy came not in old time by the will of man; but holy men spake from God, being moved by the Holy Spirit" (2 Pet. 1:19–21, 1911 Version). "Daniel the prophet," as our Lord calls him, was one of these; and his book was doubtless in Jaddua's hand—not written by some unknown apocryphal romancist a hundred years later, as modern pseudo-critics would have us believe— but a part of the inspired word of God outlining events that were coming upon the earth long before some of the nations and many of the persons specified so distinctly were in existence.

(Under the Macedonian or Greek Empire B.C. 230. to the end of the hereditary priesthood)

The "Scripture of truth," communicated to Daniel by the angel (Dan. 10:21), gives in outline the history of the wars following the death of Alexander the Great, but tells us nothing of the various high priests who succeeded one another as temporal and spiritual lords in Judea. They were frequently but the puppets of their imperial masters, whether Syrian or Egyptian; for Palestine throughout nearly a century was an almost continual battle-ground, between the Kings of the North, (Syrian) and the Kings of the South (Egyptian) in their successive wars.

Alexander died at Babylon, B.C. 323, being only about 33 years of age, after a reign of 12½ years. His was a life of remarkable achievement and marvellous conquests. With plans for greater things still to be accomplished, he died a sacrifice to his passions, when he ought to have been in the prime of manly vigor.

Having appointed no successor, nor given directions as to the disposition of his vast and newly-formed empire, with no heir but the prospect of a a yet unborn child, he left all in confusion. Disorder, intrigue, and ambition threatened to destroy the immense empire erected at so bloody a cost.

SHECHEM, BETWEEN MTS. EBAL AND GERIZIM. "*A land of hills and valleys*" (Deut. 11:11)

After a time, however, it was agreed among his principal generals that the empire should be held by them for the posthumous child, who proved to be a son and was called Alexander II. Another reputed son, Hercules, had been slain sometime before. The jealousies of the generals soon resulted in the same fate being meted out to the infant heir and his mother Roxana.

The dominions were then divided among the principal generals, only two of whom need particularly occupy us, as they are the progenitors of the two rival dynasties denominated the Kings of the North and of the South.

Antigonus, one of Alexander's most powerful generals, together with his son Demetrius seized Syria and the adjacent region, and sought to control Palestine of which Ptolemy Lagus, another general, was governor. The Jews favored Antigonus, and Ptolemy's son, Soter, determined to wreak upon them a fearful vengeance for their treasonable actions. He besieged and sacked Jerusalem, entering it on the Sabbath, massacred vast numbers of the wretched inhabitants, and transported many more (some say, one hundred thousand) to Egypt, where he gave them such unexpected privileges that, despite all they had suffered from him, they were quite content to dwell in his land, and many of their co-religionists joined them, as life in Egypt was far more peaceful than in war-torn Palestine. These Egyptian Jews became largely Gentilized as the years went on, discarding their native tongue and many of their former customs, speaking the Greek language and copying the ways of the nations. Henceforth they became a power to be reckoned with, and for a time threatened to completely annihilate the ancient Jewish faith.

Against Ptolemy Soter, Antigonus now turned his arms, and at first was successful in wresting the three provinces from him. But, for five years, triumph alternately turned between first Ptolemy then Antigonus, until the unhappy land of Palestine was about ruined, and its people completely crushed.

Many in their despair imagined that the only possible and logical way out of their distresses was to become assimilated with the warring factions of one side or the other, as much as possible; and because of Ptolemy's superior enlightenment and hopeful inducements the majority clung to him.

But in these dark days, during which Palestine was "the Debatable Land," spoiled by her warring foes, there was always an election of grace, who held tightly to the now completed Scriptures of the Old Testament, embraced under three great heads, or divisions, viz., "The Law, the Prophets and the Psalms," and clung desperately to the apparently forlorn hope of the coming Deliverer. It was of such that Malachi had written: "They that feared the Lord spake often one to another, and the Lord harkened and heard it; and a book of remembrance was written before Him for them that feared the Lord, and that thought upon His name. And they shall be mine, saith the Lord of hosts, in that day when I make up my jewels (or, peculiar treasure); and I will spare them as a man spareth his own son that serveth him. Then shall ye return and discern between the righteous and the wicked, between him that serveth God and him that serveth Him not" (Mal. 3:16–18). It was just such a separating or winnowing process that was then going on. Ptolemy and Antigonus were but the flails used to separate the wheat from the chaff, or the great rollers that crushed the ore, and freed God's jewels from the mass of the Jews in whom was but a traditional faith.

Nor were the sorrows of the remnant at an end when, in B.C. 301, the Battle of Ipsus put a quietus on the evil energy of Antigonus. In this great conflict—one of the decisive battles of the world—Antigonus and Demetrius were opposed by the renowned quartette of Alexander's generals, among whom his empire was ultimately divided, namely: Ptolemy Soter, Seleucus, Lysimachus, and Cassander. The allies were triumphant, slaying Antigonus, utterly routing his army, and causing Demetrius to flee for his life. He was apprehended several years later by Seleucus, and died in captivity.

The confederate generals, who had previously borne the titles of governors or satraps, now partitioned the empire, Cassander becoming king of Greece; Lysimachus of Thrace, or Armenia; Seleucus, of Syria and the adjacent regions; and Ptolemy of Egypt, Palestine, Libya and Arabia. It was the four-fold division of the Grecian empire pictured in the four horns of the rough goat seen in the vision by Daniel, and so plainly predicted in the "writing of truth." In fact, the eleventh chapter of Daniel gives a summary of the conflicts of the Seleucidæ (as the successors of Seleucus were called) and the Ptolemies (the Egyptian rulers) for a century and a half after the battle of Ipsus.

But as it is rather the Jews than their Gentile rulers with whom we are concerned, we turn to trace again what little is left on record of their vicissitudes while the potsherds of the earth strove with one another.

Jaddua, the high-priest, died sometime between Alexander's death and the agreement, about twenty years later, of which we have spoken. He was succeeded by Onias I., of whom we know but little, who, in turn, died B.C. 300, one year after the battle of Ipsus. His son, known as Simon the Just, succeeded him—so-called, Josephus tells us, "because of his piety toward God and his kind disposition to those of his own nation." The 50th chapter of the apocryphal book of Ecclesiasticus is his best memorial. There he is described as "Simon the high-priest, the son of Onias, who in his life repaired the house again, and in his days fortified the temple; and by him was built from the foundation the double height, the high fortress of the wall about the temple." And various other works of piety are credited to him. He is eulogized in terms that more befit Messiah Himself, even described as the "morning star," "the sun shining upon the temple," and "the rainbow giving light in the bright clouds."

That the temple service was had in honor, and a measure of reverence and godliness preserved among the priests and people in his days, must be the conclusion of all who read the chapter through.

Simon was one who sought to stem the Hellenizing or Grecianizing spirit, and to recall the people to that separation to God which would have been their strength had they known what it was to maintain it in holy humility. In verses 22 to 26 we may have the language of Jesus, the son of Sirach, but we undoubtedly have the sentiment of Simon the Just. Verses 25 and 26 are noteworthy: "There be two manner of nations which my heart abhorreth, and the third is no nation. They that sit upon the mountain of Samaria, and they that dwell among the Philistines, and that foolish people that dwell in Sichem (Shechem)."

The dwellers in Shechem, whom he stigmatizes so bitterly, were the Samaritans, who had built their hated rival temple upon Mount Gerizim, and had with abhorrent effrontery dared to add an eleventh commandment to the law: "Thou shalt build an altar on Mount Gerizim, and there only shalt thou worship!" How apt we all are, unconsciously, to arrogate such pretentious claims to that with which we have decided to associate ourselves.

The other two classes were the temporizers who sought a league with these Samaritans, and the apostates who had gone over to Israel's ancient foes, the Philistines; both alike were thorns in the side of the pious and patriotic. To the fourth party belonged Simon himself; those who repudiated all that was foreign to the spirit of Judaism and clung tenaciously to the holy writings and the sacred temple services. That these largely drifted into ceremonialism and heady exclusiveism should be a sad warning to those who attempt to maintain divine truth in a fleshly way, without the Spirit's power. From these arose the sect of the Pharisees; rigid separatists, but hard and legal, having "a form of godliness, but denying the power thereof." On the other hand, we see in the Hellenizers the forerunners of the contemptuous, cultured, but unsound Sadducees of our Lord's day.

Simon was president of the Sanhedrim or High Council of the Jews, and the first of the great Rabbis whose oral teaching was embodied in the *Mishna*, which almost superseded the word of God itself. Alas, how ready are well-meaning people to put the ministry of human teachers in the place of the Holy Scriptures, and almost unconsciously begin "teaching for doctrines the commandments of men." That Simon himself never contemplated this is evident; for, if tradition speaks truly, he it was who added the finishing touches to the work accredited to Ezra, and established authoritatively the canon of the Old Testament. He ever emphasized the supreme importance of the word of God, though he himself was looked up to in later days as if among the inspired, and in this we have another serious lesson for our own times. For there is the constant danger of either setting aside God-given teachers, or else actually allowing their ministry to supersede the Bible. Such men would indeed be the last to wish that such a place be given them. The object of all divinely-gifted servants of God would be to assert the authority of *Scripture*; their one desire in oral or written ministry would be the elucidation of the Word, and recalling the people of God to the Book, in place of giving them a substitute for it. But again and again has the ministry of great gifts, justly valued, been put in place of the Word of the living God, and thus made into a creed, which to maintain is to be orthodox, and to vary from is to be accounted heterodox.

The death of Simon the Just occurred in 291 B.C. He left an infant son; so his brother Eleazar was honored with the high-priesthood, a position he held until his death fifteen years later. Though wars abounded about them, and rumors of wars distracted them, the Jews enjoyed comparative peace in his time. The rival kings of the North and the South might carry on their struggles as they would, but Jehovah was to His people, during the reigns of the first three Ptolemies, who exercised suzerainty over Palestine, "a little sanctuary," in which the righteous found safety and peace. God was watching over them. His good hand was upon them, and they found blessing, both temporal and spiritual, though the heathen raged without, and sects within threatened eventual ruin.

Ptolemy Soter reigned twenty years, and was succeeded, 284 B.C., by his son, known as Ptolemy Philadelphus. Considerable importance attaches to his reign; for it was while he was king and Eleazar high-priest, that the first translation of the Holy Scriptures was made. The Pentateuch, or five books of Moses was, by his request, translated into Greek, about the year 277 B.C., and book after book followed until the entire Old Testament was rendered in the same language, and deposited in the Imperial Library at Alexandria. This translation is generally known as the Septuagint (seventy), from a tradition that it was the joint production of seventy translators, though it is generally supposed the correct number was seventy-two. Another tradition says it was so-named because of the idea of the Jews that there were just seventy Gentile nations, and as Greek was at that time the world-language, this was the Bible for the entire seventy.

The version thus produced rapidly grew in favor even among the Jews, few of whom could read their own Hebrew Scriptures "as the Hebrew was already fast becoming a dead language. This was the Bible used in the days of our Lord and His apostles; and largely accounts for apparent discrepancies between Old Testament texts and New Testament quotations, which are generally from the Septuagint. This Greek translation of the Old Testament is often expressed by the Roman numerals LXX.

In later days the strictly orthodox Rabbis of the Pharisaic school bitterly regretted this translation, and declared that it was "as great a calamity as the making of the golden calf." This was because some of its renderings were rather paraphrases than translations, and were of such a character as to be a great aid to the Hellenizing Jews in their efforts to introduce the new learning and to overthrow the so-called orthodox teaching.

Upon Eleazar's death, 276 B.C., his brother Manasseh became high-priest, and held office until his own decease, 251 B.C., which was the thirty-fourth year of Ptolemy Philadelphus. Little of moment occurred during his incumbency. He was succeeded by Onias II., the son of Simon the Just, who was an infant at his father's death. This man was an unworthy son of so worthy a father. Josephus describes him as "a man of little soul." During the reign of Ptolemy Eurgetes, who came to the throne 247 B.C., the evil behaviour of Onias brought the nation of the Jews into grave trouble and danger. He neglected the annual tribute of twenty talents of silver for some years until the amount due to Eurgetes became exceedingly high; and at last he sent an official called Athenion to demand the entire sum, or threaten the destruction of the Jewish state.

Onias and the inhabitants of Jerusalem were panic-stricken and knew not what to do. Only through the diplomacy of a nephew of the high-priest, Joseph, son of Tobias, was the calamity averted. He opened his house to the Egyptian ambassador and entertained him in a magnificent manner, and so pleaded for the Jews that Athenion returned to his royal master to give a most favorable report of the young man, and to counsel consideration for his nation. Joseph himself set out after him to plead in person for the royal clemency. On the way he traveled in a caravan of merchants from Cœle-Syria and Phœnicia. Overhearing certain of those declaring their business, he determined to outwit them. It was their object to endeavor to purchase from the king for eight thousand talents the right to farm the taxes throughout Cœle-Syria, Phœnicia, Judea and Samaria. Joseph saw how he might profit by such an appointment if he could obtain it for himself, so he determined to offer double the amount for the privilege, depending upon more than making it up out of the people. On the proper occasion he made his offer and was able to secure the position, and two thousand men were appointed to assist him. He was thus the first Jewish publican—the beginning of a detestable class in the eyes of all lovers of Israel, and put on the same level as the "sinners" of the nations, or even considered beneath them.

For twenty-two years Joseph kept this place. For a time, during the ascendency of Antiochus the Great (of whose wars we shall speak later on), he lost his lucrative post, but recovered it again when the Egyptian arms triumphed, and held it until his death.

We can well understand the abhorrence that Joseph's course would inspire in the breasts of true Jewish patriots. As the servant of a foreign potentate, and under his protection, he enriched himself at the expense of his own people, grinding the faces of the poor, and extorting from them all he possibly could by taxes on their lands and goods, of which he kept for himself all that was over and above the yearly fee paid to the king of Egypt for the privilege. No wonder the name "publican" came to be a synonym for all that was disgraceful to the Jew, and unworthy.

Upon the demise of Onias II., his son Simon II., succeeded him as high priest.

In his days grave conflicts were continually going on among the nations around, but there was comparative peace in Judea, save that warring factions among themselves did much to disturb the equanimity of the Jewish commonwealth. Particularly was this the case between the family of Joseph, known as "the sons of Tobias," and the house of the high-priest. The ill-gotten gains of the publican-priest brought joy neither to himself nor his family, but resulted in a household feud of fiercest intensity, into the details of which we need not now enter, but shall advert to later.

The kings of the North and South continued their struggle for the possession of the Land, and once more Palestine played the part of a "buffer state."

Seleucus Nicator, the founder of the dynasty of the *Seleucidæ*, reigned thirty-three years, and was succeeded by Antiochus Soter, who reigned nineteen years. His successor, Antiochus Theos, wedded Berenice, a daughter of Ptolemy Philadelphus, who hoped thereby to strengthen his hold on Syria, but the ruse was a failure, and only made matters worse.

Antiochus Theos was followed by Seleucus Callinicus. He was killed, 226 B.C., by a fall from his horse. This was the year after Onias II sent his crafty nephew Joseph into Egypt to make peace with Ptolemy. Seleucus Ceraunas, a weakling, and an object of contempt, succeeded Callinicus, but was poisoned within a short time. He was succeeded by his brother, destined to become one of the most renowned of the

Syrian kings, and known in history as Antiochus the Great. He became king 223 B.C., while Ptolemy Euergetes was on the Egyptian throne. This prince died two years later, poisoned, it is supposed, by his son Ptolemy IV., known as Philopater, who soon afterwards murdered his mother and brother. Against him Antiochus the Great declared war, with the ostensible purpose of recovering Palestine and the adjacent lands for himself. At first he was successful, but at the battle of Raphia, 217 B.C., he was defeated with tremendous loss.

Philopater marched through the land in triumph, and the people everywhere submitted to the exultant victor. In Jerusalem he gained the favor of the Jews by giving rich gifts to the temple and offering many sacrifices and oblations. But he undid all this a little later by insisting upon entering the Holy of holies against the vehement protests of priests and people. Tradition says that as he impiously pressed forward he was smitten with paralysis and carried out half dead. As a result, he left Judea in dismay, but with intense hatred for all things Jewish.

A peace was shortly afterwards patched up between Ptolemy and Antiochus, whereby Cœle-Syria and Palestine were confirmed to the king of Egypt. For a few years following, the Jews in Palestine had rest, but it was far otherwise with those who were settled in Alexandria and other parts of Egypt. Against them the resentment of Ptolemy burned fiercely, and he persecuted them unmercifully, thus proving that Egypt was, as the prophet had long ago declared, "a bruised reed" to rest upon.

Philopater died 204 B.C., succeeded by his son Ptolemy Epiphanes, a child of but five years of age. In his minority Antiochus the Great re-asserted his claim to the lost territories, and seized them in 203–2, B.C. A few years later Scopas, an Egyptian general, led an army into Palestine and recovered the two provinces, but the following year, 198 B.C., Antiochus recaptured them. In 193 B.C., a marriage was consummated between the youthful Ptolemy and Cleopatra, daughter of Antiochus, and on the basis of this a peaceful agreement entered into whereby the revenues should be divided between the two kingdoms, and Palestine be nominally subject to Egypt. On Antiochus' further troubles, his war with Rome, his defeat, his sacrilegious pillaging of the temple of Jupiter-Belus (187 B.C.), and his death by the hands of the mob, when according to Daniel's words, "He stumbled and fell, and was not found," we need not here dwell, as it is with the Jews we are immediately concerned.

Their sufferings had been fearful to contemplate in the awful years referred to above. Whichever party won, *they* lost. Whoever prospered, *they* were *robbed*. But in those days of terror and nights of anguish, who can doubt that "many were purified and made white" who otherwise would have been living in ease and careless indifference toward God?

Seleucus Philopater followed his father as king of Syria, but died by the treachery of his treasurer, Heliodorus, 175 B.C. This Seleucus is the "raiser of taxes" spoken of in Dan. 11; his father's war with Rome having made it necessary to purchase peace at a great price.

Ptolemy Epiphanes died by poison while yet a youth, 180 B.C., and his son, Ptolemy Philometer reigned in his stead; his mother, Cleopatra, being queen-regent. At this time Seleucus Philopater held authority over Palestine, though how he obtained it is not clear, but it seems that the Jews themselves preferred Syrian to Egyptian rule, and readily submitted to him. This was during the high-priesthood of Onias III., in whose days the second book of the Maccabees says, "The holy city was inhabited in all peace, and the laws were kept very well, because of the godliness of Onias, the high-priest, and his hatred of wickedness" (2 Macc. 3:1). Thus we have again illustrated the proverb, "Like priest like people." On the other hand, we have evidence of an easy-going self-confidence which rested in keeping the laws of the Lord "very well," when, in reality, there was the gravest reason to be in the dust of humiliation before God for the centuries of failure that had resulted in the *Lo-ammi* condition in which they were still found. For they are never owned as God's people after the Babylonian captivity, nor will be again till their repentance in the time of the end yet to come.

Onias III was the last to obtain the high-priesthood by inheritance. He was eventually deposed by Antiochus Epiphanes, brother and successor to Seleucus Philopater. With his setting aside, the high-priestly epoch closes and a new period begins, which we leave, with the events leading up to it, for a distinct chapter.

The century we have been considering, was one in which the Jews had practically no national history, and we have been chiefly occupied with their rulers and neighbors. They were, nevertheless, ever under the eye of

God, and nothing happened to them but what his love and wisdom allowed.

Throughout all the darkness, He kept a lamp of testimony burning in Jerusalem, according to the word He had sworn to His servants of old, for David's sake and for His own glory.

In the next period He gave them unexpected deliverances that remind us of the days of the Judges, and to the consideration of this heroic epoch we will now turn.[3]

---

[3] I have endeavored to trace out a little more in detail the history of the Ptolemies and the Seleucidae in my Lectures on Daniel. The inquiring reader might consult the address on chapter 11:1-35.

II. The Days of the Maccabees

FOR long time there had been two main parties striving for the domination in Judea: One, and that the weaker company, clinging tenaciously to the law and its observance, though continually adding to it, and becoming more and more legal. These eventually became known as the Pharisees from a root meaning *to separate*), and whom the apostle Paul describes long after this as "the straitest sect of our religion," and whose self-righteousness and hypocrisy the Lord had to condemn so severely in His days on earth. Only by degrees, of course, and after a long time did the Jewish party reach the condition depicted in the New Testament. It was the result of holding the truth in a carnal way—contending for what was divine while neglecting spiritually and self-judgment. They thus became censorious judges of others and complacent condoners of themselves.

On the other hand, the dominant party in the days of Simon II and Onias III was the Hellenizing faction—bringing in Grecian ways and customs. They saw no deliverance for the Jews save in following the ways of the nations. They cried, "Let us go and make a covenant with the heathen" (1 Macc. 1:11), and sought to popularize as far as possible the new ways. Greek philosophy, Greek games, and even tolerance of Greek religion were persistently advocated. Even Onias II., the high-priest, had been suspected of thus trying to break down the middle wall of separation; and later priests openly confessed their desire to see all that was distinctively Jewish replaced by what was Grecian. These were the predecessors of the polished, but infidel Sadducees.

HELIODORUS DRIVEN FROM THE TEMPLE

Besides these two great parties, there was a third, if it be right to stigmatize them by the appellation *party*. They were a feeble and, afflicted people, "the poor of the flock," who abhorred the ways of the heathen, yet refused the legal pretensions of the Nationalists, and clung devotedly to the word of God and the promise of the coming Messiah. From these sprang, in after-years, the Essenes—a sect whose actual tenets are difficult to define, but who placed spirituality above outward conformity. They have been called the Quakers of Judea, and by others the Pietists.

But there were also purely political factions disturbing the peace of Judea. An "Egyptian" and a "Syrian" party had been gradually developed among the Jews, the names plainly indicating the object of each. In addition to these features of unrest, corruption had made sad inroads among the priesthood and the heads of the people. Avarice and covetousness, love of power and of ease, were eating the very life out of the great families and those who should have been examples to the flock.

We have already mentioned Joseph, the son of Tobias, who first bought the privilege of farming the taxes from Ptolemy Eurgetes. This lucrative office was held by him and his sons for many years, giving them thereby an importance almost as great as that of the high-priest. But the love of money is a root for all evils, and it brought disaster to the house of Tobias. Joseph was the husband of two wives, one of whom bore him seven sons; the other, but one, who was named Hyrcanus. The father's own character was thoroughly reproduced in this youth, in greed and cunning. In his father's old age, he was sent by him to Egypt to congratulate the king and queen on the birth of a son. Hyrcanus used the opportunity to bribe the king with money obtained from his father's agent, and by these unworthy means secured the royal authority to become collector of revenues on the east of Jordan. This greatly enraged his father Joseph and his brothers, who waylaid Hyrcanus and sought to kill him. They were themselves defeated, however, and two of them slain, while Hyrcanus escaped unharmed. Joseph did not long survive this event. After his death matters went from bad to worse.

The strife overleaped the family of Tobias and became a national affair. Some of the people, amongst whom was Simon the high-priest, espoused the cause of the five brothers, while others supported Hyrcanus, who retreated beyond Jordan, and seven years later committed suicide, fearing the wrath of Antiochus, the Syrian king, who then held sway over the land. Before he died, he appears to have obtained the favor of Onias III., the last hereditary high-priest (who succeeded Simon his father, 195 B.C), for the ill-gotten treasure of Hyrcanus was deposited in the temple, and Onias described the publican as "a man of great dignity."

At this time the governor of the temple was a Simon who is supposed to have been the eldest brother of Hyrcanus. Between him and Onias a bitter feud developed, and in 176 B.C., Simon, finding Onias too powerful for him to cope with in Jerusalem, went to Apollonius, governor of all that region (under Seleucus Philopater, the "raiser of taxes," of whom we have spoken in the previous chapter), and told him of the immense treasure of Hyrcanus and others deposited for safe-keeping in the sanctuary.

Apollonius lost no time in acquainting the king with the welcome news, and the needy monarch at once sent Heliodorus, his treasurer, to take possession of the money. In some way he was hindered, and the treasure was not removed. The story told in 2 Macc. 3:5–40 is that Heliodorus came to Jerusalem and made inquiry of Onias, who informed him that the treasure was indeed there, but that it would be sacrilege to touch it. The king's treasurer, however, demanded the money, and upon his being denied he attempted to enter the temple to secure it, when he saw an apparition in the form of "a horse with a terrible rider upon him, and adorned with a very fair covering, and he ran fiercely, and smote at Heliodorus with his forefeet, and it seemed that he that sat upon the horse had complete harness of gold. Moreover two other young men appeared before him, notable in strength, excellent in beauty, and comely in apparel, who stood by him at either side, and scourged him continually, and gave him many sore stripes" (2

Macc. 3:25, 26). This turned the treasurer from his purpose, and he departed to his master without the object of his quest.

It is related, however, that Simon was not so credulous as Heliodorus, but boldly insinuated trickery, and declared that Onias was responsible in some way for the supposed apparition. Bitterness and strife increased; partisans were assassinated, and dissension grew so intolerable that Onias departed on a mission to the king, determined to secure his intervention. Things had fallen to a low ebb indeed when a heathen monarch had thus to be appealed to with a view to settling a dispute among the descendants of those zealous Jews returned out of Babylonish captivity in the days of Zerubbabel and Nehemiah.

Seleucus, the king, died, however, before Onias reached him, and the king's brother, Antiochus, who surnamed himself *Epiphanes* (the illustrious), was declared king. He is called by an opposite designain Daniel 11:21, R. V., namely, "a contemptible person." His own courtiers evidently concurred in this last appellation, for they changed one Greek letter in this self-assumed name, which made it *Epimanes* (the *madman).*

This wretched king is the persecuting "King of the North," a synopsis of whose history had been pre-written in Daniel 11:21–35. He has been well-named "The Antichrist of the Old Testament." At first he came in peaceably, and by flatteries sought to gain the confidence of the Jews, but afterwards became their bitterest persecutor, and the profaner of the temple. Ere Onias could gain his ear, Joshua, the high-priest's brother, offered this Antiochus four hundred and forty talents in all if he would sell him the high-priestly position, and set aside his venerable brother. Joshua further promised to do all in his power toward Grecianizing the Jews, even to the changing their name to "Antiochians." This offer delighted the avaricious ruler, who declared Onias no longer high-priest, but gave the office to Joshua, who at once began to carry out his pledges, giving up his own honored name for that of Jason, after a Greek hero. He constructed a gymnasium, and furthered in every way the adoption of Greek learning, fashions and games; even going "so far as to send special messengers from Jerusalem to Tyre bearing money for offerings to Melcarth, the Phœnician Hercules, on the occasion of the games in his honor" (see 2 Macc. 4:18–20).

Thus was the rationalistic pre-Sadducean party completely in power, and it seemed as though both the national and the spiritual parties were thoroughly crushed, if not ready to be annihilated. The first chapter of the first book of the Maccabees gives us a vivid picture of the wretched estate of the Jews, who had begun so well under Ezra and his coadjutors.

Four years passed, and Jason, the pseudo-priest, sent a younger brother named Onias, to Antioch, bearing the tribute-money for Antiochus. Jason now was to prove that "whatsoever a man soweth, that shall he also reap." He had sown deceit and treachery through flattery and bribery. He reaped the same. For Onias determined to obtain the lucrative and honorable title of high-priest for himself. He therefore flattered and fawned upon the vain, covetous king, and offered him three hundred talents more than Jason for the position. He was successful, therefore, and returned to Jerusalem, bearing the royal commission, with the intention of ousting his brother from the office. The "sons of Tobias" rallied to his support, but Jason and his friends refused to relinquish their place and power, so that Onias was forced to retire to Antioch, temporarily outwitted. There he besought the king's aid, pledging himself to go further than his brother in Grecianizing the Jews, and changing his own name to Menelaus. This won the king to hearty support of his cause, and he returned once more to Jerusalem with a royal escort. At this Jason fled in terror and Menelaus held the priesthood.

The senior Onias, the last legitimate high-priest, still lived, and "vexed his righteous soul" as he saw the evil deeds of the apostate party. Finally, when Menelaus, in order to make up the tribute-money, robbed the temple of its golden vessels, selling them at Tyre and elsewhere, Onias sternly spoke out, calling the false priest to account for his unhallowed ways. For this he was hated by the sacrilegious wretch whom he had reproved, and he appointed Andronicus to assassinate him. The aged pontiff was foully murdered, and Menelaus congratulated himself on having his stern reprover out of the way. But the vile deed inflamed many lovers of Israel, and so great a protest was made to Antiochus, that he felt compelled to interfere by causing Andronicus to be put to death, though Menelaus himself escaped. As time went by he became more and more abandoned, reveling in shameful iniquity, and guilty of horrible enormities—yet wearing the sacred mitre inscribed with "Holiness unto the Lord!"

Again he laid hands on other of the holy vessels, but this time the mass of the people, among whom were ever found many who "looked for redemption in Israel," rose up in their wrath, determined to defend the house of

God against this sacrilegious plunderer. They joined battle with three thousand of the partisans of Menelaus, led by Lysimachus his brother. Lysimachus was killed and his party defeated. Menelaus chagrined and disgraced appealed to the king, sending a delegation of rationalistic members of the Sanhedrim bearing the most potent of arguments—money in abundance. The people protested, but all their complaints were ignored at the sight of Menelaus' gold, and the king acquitted the high-priest and slew his accusers.

Antiochus Epiphanes invaded Egypt, about 171 B.C., and soon a rumor reached Jerusalem that he was dead. Upon the circulation of this report there was great rejoicing, and the Jason party again gathered courage, knowing that the people detested Menelaus. With a thousand men they carried the walls, slew their opponents, and drove Menelaus into the castle. But a sudden turn of affairs enabled the latter to get the upper hand, and Jason was driven out and retreated to a strange land, where he died "detested by all," as one historian says, and as we can well believe.

News that Jerusalem had been overjoyed to hear of his death reached Antiochus in Egypt and threw him into a fury. The troubles between Jason and Menelaus were reported as though there had been a popular uprising and a revolt against the royal authority. In a paroxysm of rage he led his armies like an overwhelming flood through the land, and assaulting Jerusalem with wrathful energy, took the city by storm, upon which followed a fearful sack and carnage. Over 40,000 persons were slain in three days, and an equal number torn from their homes and led away as captives. Nor was this all. Guided by the wretched apostate Menelaus, he forced his way into the

Holiest of all, carried off the golden candlestick, the table, the incense altar, and other vessels; destroyed the books of the law, and set up the "abomination of desolation" by erecting an idol-altar upon the holy altar of burnt-offerings, upon which he sacrificed a great sow, and with a broth made of its unclean flesh, sprinkled and defiled all the temple.

The horror with which a godly Jew regarded this terrible desecration is almost beyond our conception. Never till the personal Antichrist sits in the temple of God yet to be erected in Jerusalem, in the days of the coming tribulation, will such dreadful scenes be repeated. Both are called by the same name. In Daniel 11:31 the *past deed* is depicted years before the event: "And armed men going forth from him shall pollute the sanctuary, the fortress, and shall take away the continual sacrifice, and they shall set up the abomination that maketh desolate." In Daniel 9:26, 27, *the future* is before us, when the Antichrist will again defile the temple, "and for the overspreading of abominations he shall make it desolate." This is what Daniel 12:11 refers to, and is the passage to which our Lord directed the attention of His disciples in Matt. 24:15, as a sign of the end of the age.

The impious acts of Antiochus became a signal for the revival of the ancient spirit in a remnant, according to Daniel 11:32: "And such as do wickedly against the covenant shall he corrupt by flatteries; but the people that do know their God shall be strong and do exploits." Thus the Maccabean period is introduced—the time of the great Jewish war of independence. Then it was that the following verses, 33 to 35, were literally fulfilled:[4] "And they that have understanding among the people shall instruct many; yet they shall fall by the sword, and by flame, by captivity, and by spoil many days. Now when they shall fall they shall be helped with a little help: but many shall join themselves to them with flatteries. And some of them of understanding shall fall, to try them, and to purify, and to make them white, even to the time of the end: because it is yet for a time appointed."

For twenty-three hundred days, or about six and a half years, the temple was to be polluted, according to the same prophet Daniel. Then the sanctuary was to be cleansed and divine service re-instituted. And so it was. In 171 B.C. the abomination that made desolate was set up. In 165–4 B.C. the temple was purified and re-dedicated by command of Judas Maccabeus. The intervening 2300 days were the strenuous times of which we now proceed to take note.

For a time the Jews were utterly disheartened, yet a remnant cried to God: "O Lord, how long?" and hoped in Him who had ever been the Helper of Israel.

In 169 B.C. Antiochus made another inroad against Egypt, and was at first successful, until met by a Roman embassage demanding that he return to his own land. The decree of the Roman senate was handed to the haughty tyrant, who asked for time to consider it; but with his rod, Popillius, one of the ambassadors, drawing

---

[4] The reader will observe that this concludes the past history of the Jews in Daniel 11. Verse 36, which has not yet come to pass, refers to the days of Antichrist. (See the author's Lectures on Daniel.)

a circle around Antiochus, demanded an answer of yes or no before he left the circle. Antiochus, alarmed, submitted and left Egypt, determined to vent his rage on Palestine again. He sent an army under Apollonius to destroy the already ruined city of Jerusalem, the name of which signifies "Foundation of peace," but which has known more sieges and bloodshed than any other existing city— having been sacked twenty-seven times already, and God's word clearly predicts two fearful sieges for the future.

Apollonius fell upon the defenceless people in a manner worthy of the madman he served. Pretending peace, he entered unopposed, and on the holy Sabbath day fell upon the wretched inhabitants, slaying the men by thousands, and carrying the women and children captive. The houses and walls were demolished and the city set on fire. Thus, in the pathetic language of 1 Macc. 1:39, "Her sanctuary was laid waste like a wilderness; her feasts were turned into mourning, her Sabbaths into reproach, her honor into contempt."

And over and above all this an Act of Uniformity was passed compelling all the people in the dominions of Antiochus to worship his gods and no others. Athenseus was sent to Jerusalem to dedicate the temple to Jupiter Olympus, in whose honor sacrifices were instituted, and the miserable Jews still remaining among the ruins of their old homes were forced to take part in the horrid services and to eat of the unclean sacrifices. Defilement could not further go. Israel had been made to know to the full the tender mercies of the heathen, whose culture and brilliancy had been so attractive to the rationalizers among them. The outward contamination was but the manifestation of what God's holy eye had seen long since; even as the leprosy on king Uzziah's forehead had but made known before all the corruption that had been working within.

Antiochus and his minions knew no mercy. They spared neither age, sex, nor condition. Young and old, men and women, priests and people, rich and poor, suffered alike in those fearful days of vengeance. Women who attempted to keep the law and circumcise their sons, were led publicly through the city with their babes at their breasts and flung bodily from the city walls, thus being literally broken to pieces. Any who were discovered observing the Sabbath day were apprehended and burnt alive.

Josephus' account of those dire and sorrowful times remarkably coincides with the epistle to the Hebrews' account of former saints' sufferings. Says the Jewish historian: "They were whipped with rods, and their bodies were torn to pieces, and were crucified while they were still alive and breathed." The apostle wrote of the same heroes of faith: "They were tortured, not accepting deliverance, that they might obtain a better resurrection; and others had trial of cruel mockings and scourgings, yea, moreover of bonds and imprisonment. They were stoned, they were sawn asunder, were tempted, were slain with the sword: they wandered about in sheepskins and goatskins; being destitute, afflicted, tormented (*of whom the world was not worthy*); they wandered in deserts and mountains, and dens and caves of the earth" (Heb. 11:35–38).

One incident will show how truly these words applied to the faithful among the Jews in this time of trouble. One woman and her seven sons were apprehended together and dragged before the vile and infamous king, who commanded them to cast off their faith and to become worshipers of his gods. As they boldly refused, the first son was seized in the presence of his heroic mother and his six brethren, his tongue torn out, his members cut off, and he burned alive over a slow fire. Again the alternative was presented to worship the demon-gods and live, or be faithful to Jehovah and die. Unyielding, the second son was taken and flayed alive before the eyes of the rest. And so the horrid trial went on till but one son was left, and he the youngest. The king personally pleaded with him to renounce his faith and bow to the gods, promising riches, ease and honor for himself and his mother if he obeyed. Fearing he might weaken, the devoted woman encouraged his heart in the Lord, saying, "O my son, have pity upon me that bare thee ... I beseech thee, my son, look upon heaven and earth, and all that is therein, and consider that God made them of things that were not; and so was mankind made likewise. Fear not this tormentor, but be worthy of thy brethren; take thy death, that I may receive thee again in mercy with thy brethren" (2 Macc. 7:27–29). How strong was this testimony to the Jewish faith in the resurrection when uncorrupted by Sadducean influence!

The youth, thus encouraged, defied the king, rebuked him for his iniquity, and predicted his final judgment, till the wretched monarch was so enraged that, we are told, he "handled him worse than all the rest," and "this man died undefiled, and put his whole trust in the Lord" (chap. 7:39, 40). The mother was then despatched, and the eight faithful spirits rested together in Abraham's bosom.

It would only be soul-harrowing to dwell longer on details such as these. The night was indeed dark; the storm raged relentlessly; hope almost died within the breasts of the faithful; when, like the shining forth of the star of morning, arose Mattathias who dwelt in Modin.

This man was the father of five sons, and he and his sons are the Maccabees of everlasting renown. The name means, "The hammer of God," and was originally the appellation given to the third son Judas, but is generally now applied to them all.

It is not possible at this late day to locate the village of Modin, where dwelt this devoted family of priestly descent. Mattathias was of the house of Asmonæus, of the course of Joarib, so his family are called Asmonæas. They were among those who bewailed before God the corruption and violence of the times, and in secret were being prepared by the mighty One in whom they trusted, for public service.

There came one day to Modin, Apelles, king Antiochus' commissioner, to force all the inhabitants to conform to the heathen rites. Recognizing in Mattathias a ruler and an honorable man, Apelles came first to him, demanding that he set the example by sacrificing on the heathen altar which had been set up in the midst of the village. Mattathias indignantly refused, and declared without reservation that neither he nor his sons would harken to the king's words. As he spoke, a renegade Jew pressed through the throng to offer before the idol. This so stirred the venerable old man that he ran forward and slew not only the transgressor himself, but ere the astonished commissioner realized his danger, he also was slain by Mattathias, who then destroyed the altar. Thus had a second Phinehas arisen in Israel.

The breach was made; the king was openly defied. So, crying, "Whosoever is zealous of the law, and maintaineth the covenant, let him follow me," the aged Mattathias fled from the city into a mountain retreat, leaving all his goods behind him. Unto him, as to David in the hold, a company of devoted men gathered, his own sons leading the way. So had God again visited the Jews, even in the days when they were still under the *Lo-ammi* sentence—"Not My people"—because of their sins. The flame of insurrection spread far and wide, and as of old, the "discontented, in debt, and distressed," rallied to the standard of Mattathias.

From Jerusalem an army of Syrians was at once despatched to crush the rebellion in its very inception. They fell upon a heterogeneous mass of Jews who were encamped in the wilderness, on their way to the hiding place of Mattathias. It was the holy Sabbath, and the patriotic band felt they dared not violate its sanctity by armed resistance, so a thousand were butchered like defenceless sheep. But this led to a change of judgment, and decided the Jews never again to refuse to defend their country and their families on the holy day, but to fight manfully for all that was dearer to them than life itself, even on the Sabbath, the rest of which had been so rudely disturbed by the ferocious heathen.

The most devoted Jews joined Mattathias; those known as the Assidæans, or Chasidim (*i. e.*, the Pious), who detested all that savored of idolatry, and clung tenaciously to the old paths, as well as the nationalist party, who were actuated more by mere patriotism than true piety.

From place to place this band of insurrectionists went through the country, daily augmented by fresh recruits, tearing down idol-altars, overthrowing heathen temples, circumcising the children who were without the covenant-sign, and proclaiming the triumph of the law of God.

For less than a year was Mattathias spared, the intensity of the times being too much for his years; and in 166 B.C. the venerable old patriarch died. Ere he resigned his laborious work he gathered his sons about him, and charged them not to turn aside from the service he now committed to them till the land and the temple were cleansed of the pollutions of the heathen. His son Judas, "Maccabeus" (the hammer of God), he appointed to succeed himself as leader of the revolutionary army, while he called upon all to weigh well the wise counsels of his son Simon, who was noted for his sagacity and singleness of purpose. The aged leader was buried in Modin, amid great lamentation, and at his tomb the people consecrated themselves anew to the service of God and their brethren.

Victory everywhere crowned the efforts of Judas. He surprised the enemy time after time, bursting in upon their encampments in the middle of the night, spreading terror and confusion among them, and causing himself to be dreaded by them all.

Apollonius, the governor of Samaria, went out against him with a great host, but was ignominiously defeated, and at last himself slain, while his army was scattered and their arms and accoutrements left in the hands of the Jews. With the sword of Apollonius the great Maccabean chieftain fought ever afterwards.

ANCIENT COINS

ANCIENT COINS

COIN OF PTOLEMY I. COIN OF PTOLEMY III.

COIN OF TITUS.

Another and greater army, commanded by Seron, was sent by king Antiochus to annihilate the Jewish company. The two forces met at Beth-horon. Seron, haughty and defiant, at the head of a vast host; Judas, intrepid and strong in faith, but leading a small company, who had been obliged to fast all that day, and were weak and discouraged as they beheld their insolent foes. "How," they asked, "shall we be able, being so few, to fight against so great a multitude, and so strong?" Like a second Asa, Judas replied: "With the God of heaven it is all one to deliver with a great multitude, or a small company." Nor was his faith disappointed. Encouraged by the remembrance of the past mercies of Jehovah, the Jews threw themselves, in the apparent recklessness of faith, upon their disdainful foes, and under the daring leadership of Judas, scattered them like chaff before the flails, and completely defeated the Syrians, who fled wildly in all directions, leaving a vast number of dead and wounded on the bloody field. Thus was it demonstrated that one should chase a thousand, and two put ten thousand to flight, in reliance upon God their strength.

News of these events threw Antiochus into a fury; he raged like a maniac as report of success after success on the part of Judas and his bands reached the Syrian capital. A great army was at once planned, to be led by the king in person, which would utterly annihilate the detested Jews. But money was lacking; the treasury being practically empty, the angry king set off to Persia to collect tribute, and with other means to raise the much-needed funds. Meantime, half of the army was sent to Palestine, headed by Lysias, one of his mightiest generals, who was charged to completely extirpate all Israel, and blot out of the land every memorial in existence of the insolent nation that had dared to defy so mighty a king!

It seems to have been Satan's great effort to destroy the seed of Abraham, and so to nullify the Messianic promise. Often had he sought thus to bring to nought the word of God in the past, but had been divinely defeated on every occasion; and he, the great arch-enemy of God and men, was again to find that he was powerless against the fiat of the Eternal.

Lysias divided the army among three generals, Ptolemy, Nicanor, and Gorgias, with 40,000 foot and 7,000 horsemen, sending this great host into Judea to preclude all possibility of defeat. So certain were the Syrians of victory that Nicanor had it publicly proclaimed that upon his return ninety Jews would be sold for one talent; thus arousing the cupidity of the dealers in slaves, whose money it was supposed would soon be pouring into the coffers of Antiochus.

Against this mighty army Judas could only oppose a visible force of 6,000 men; but can we doubt that the armies of heaven, visible only to faith, were encamping round about the little Jewish band, as of old in the mountains surrounding Dothan?

The Syrians pitched at Emmaus, and at Mizpeh was the camp of the Jews. With ashes on their heads and sackcloth on their bodies, they fell down before God in prayer and confession. Eleazar, the brother of Judas, read from the Holy Scriptures as they fasted and humbled themselves before the mighty One who had been their Help in ages past. He was their reliance in the hour of trial then approaching. For their battle-cry they took the words, "The help of God;" and with hearts strong in the Lord and the power of His might, they waited for the morrow.

And while they waited, they watched. Faithful sentries noted every move of the over-confident Syrians. Ere daylight scouts came to Judas to tell him that the division of the enemy under Gorgias was already preparing to march, hoping by an early attack to surprise the sleeping Jews and to carry all before them. The little army of Israel were roused at once. When Gorgias arrived at the Jewish camp he found it deserted, for Judas and his men were already marching down upon the Syrians by a different road. Suddenly the cry of Judas, "Fear ye not!" rang out on the still air, and a loud blast of trumpets sounded the assault. Like men who knew neither fear nor danger the Jews flung themselves upon the great army before them, and in a few moments the enemy were scattered in all directions. Three thousand Syrians fell, and when Gorgias returned, in ignorance of the events of the early morning, he imagined the Jews were in retreat. "These fellows flee from us," he cried, and led his band on in haste to the plain, only to find the tents on fire and the Syrians fleeing in disorder on every side. Amazed and disheartened, Gorgias and his men turned and fled as a company of Jews bore down upon them.

Thus was the battle ended, and the army of Lysias disgracefully defeated. The Jews gathered the spoil together, then rested for the Sabbath, praising God for His marvelous ways and mercy to Israel.

Determined to retrieve the good name of his army, Lysias gathered a force of nearly twenty thousand more men the following year and again descended upon Judea. But the army of Judas was now ten thousand strong, and with these zealots, relying on "the Saviour of Israel," he boldly met the 65,000 Syrians in Idumea, and drove Lysias in defeat and disgrace to Antiochia. So overwhelming was this blow, that it was years before the Syrian army recovered from its effects, and in the meantime (164 B.C), less than a year after the triumph of Judas, the vile Antiochus Epiphanes died a horrible death, raving in madness and foul with an evil disease that rotted the flesh upon his bones while life was yet in his filthy body. He had reigned eleven years, and came to his end as he was hastening home from Persia to avenge the defeat of his generals upon the exultant Jews.

But ere the king's death, an event of great importance occurred at Jerusalem: the cleansing of the temple, as predicted by Daniel, at the expiration of the 2,300 days of defilement. It was in 171 B.C. that the sanctuary was first polluted. In 165 and 164, the holy place was purified, and the ancient service reestablished amid the joyful acclamations of the Chasidim and the enthusiastic shouts of the nationalists.

When Judas and his brethren went up to Jerusalem it was a dreadful sight that greeted them. The holy city was in ruins, the temple disfigured and desolate, the courts overgrown with shrubs, the sacred altar profaned, the beautiful gate burned, and the entire place a scene of desolation. Rending their garments, the people gave way to wailing and tears, but the sound of the trumpet called them to labor, not to weep; and with a small armed company set aside to keep the Syrian garrison in the fortress in check, the rest began the labor of repairing the sanctuary and cleansing the building and the hallowed vessels. The altar was set aside altogether as too unclean for purification, and a new one built in its place. The temple was renovated and decorated, and at last, all was in readiness for its re-dedication. This took place on the 25th Chisleu, 165 B.C., exactly three years from the day when the first offering had been made on the altar to Jupiter, and some six and a half years after it had been first polluted by Antiochus. Ever after, the Jews kept "The Feast of the Dedication" as a yearly festival (see John 10:22), in the wintry month of Chisleu, or December. Ere the next year, 164 B.C., was well advanced, the temple service was going on again as before the desecration.

For the greater part of the next three years the work of ridding the land of its enemies and restoring the cities of Israel was vigorously carried on by the heroic Judas. He fortified Mount Zion and placed a Jewish garrison there, rebuilt the walls, and rehabilitated the waste places, bringing order out of chaos, and changing despair to hopeful contemplation of the future. Upon an uprising of Israel's ancient foes, the Idumeans, or Edomites, and the Ammonites, Judas and his brother Jonathan led an army into their territories and discomfited them at every turn, till they were glad to make peace and refrain from further interference. Simon, a brother of Judas, commanded an army that overran Galilee, subjugating lawless bands which were inflicting terror by pillaging and slaying the defenceless people who had sought refuge there. Wherever the Maccabean brothers were in command victory followed; but on several occasions, when led by rash and misguided men, the Jews were defeated.

Antiochus Epiphanes was succeeded by his nine-year-old son, known as Antiochus Eupator; Lysias, the old enemy of the Jews, was regent, and again he determined to wipe out the stain upon his honor by crushing Judas and his forces. He invaded the land, therefore, with an army vastly greater than that commanded by Judas. The two hosts met in Judea, and, for the first time, the Jews suffered a serious reverse. Eleazar, the brother of Judas, was slain while attempting to destroy what he supposed was the king's beast. He observed a large elephant, gorgeously bedecked, and thought it was ridden by the boy-king and his guards. Thinking to win undying renown, and to stem the assault of the foe, he cut his way through a company of Syrians, got underneath the mighty beast and thrust his spear into its belly. The great creature fell, crushing Eleazar by its weight. It was not the king's beast, however, and nothing was really accomplished by the indiscretion of Eleazar. His death greatly discouraged the

Jews, while it did not hinder the progress of the invaders, who drove their stubborn foes before them, so that they retreated to Jerusalem.

Lysias laid siege to the city, and cutting off all supplies, threatened all the inhabitants with death by famine if they attempted to hold out against him. But the God of Israel intervened again, and caused the purpose of Lysias to be frustrated by the breaking out of rebellion in Syria: Philip, a rival of Lysias, having attempted to overthrow the government in the latter's absence.

This made it imperative for Lysias to raise the siege and to return in haste to the capital; which he did, after concluding peace with the Jews, guaranteeing them protection. But when the king was admitted to the city and his officers saw the strength of the walls, the pledge was partially violated by the destruction of the defenses. The army then marched away in haste to Antiochia, where Philip was outwitted and the rebellion crushed.

It will be remembered that the treacherous highpriest Menelaus was in office when Mattathias first rose against the Syrians. He continued to hold the title through all the stormy years of revolution, but met his death at this time. Lysias, declaring that he was the real cause of the revolt, impeached him before the king. He was slain, then, and the high-priesthood conferred upon one named Alcimus, who, unfortunately, was every whit as vile as his infamous predecessor. This was in 163 B.C.

The rest of the story of Judas is soon told. During the next year he labored earnestly for the blessing of Israel, though he it was who first formed the Roman alliance as a result of which Judea became eventually a Roman province. The circumstances were these: In 162 B.C., Demetrius, son of Seleucus Philopater, and therefore nephew of Antiochus Epiphanes and cousin of Eupator, appeared in Syria to contest the authority of the boy-king. He had been carried to Rome as a hostage some years before, but had escaped and made his way to Tripolis in Syria, where he gave out that the Roman senate had authorized him to take over the kingdom from his cousin. Many rallied to his standard, and after a desperate conflict the king and Lysias were apprehended by the pretender and put to death. Demetrius then ascended the throne, taking the title Soter, meaning Saviour.

Alcimus, the newly-appointed high-priest, bought his favor with a present of a golden crown and other gifts, and thus his office was confirmed to him. This hypocritical, self-seeking prelate lost no time in slandering Judas Maccabæus and his followers to the king, and command was given to Nicanor, the old enemy of the Jewish commonwealth, to advance against Judas, put him to death, and destroy his army. But Nicanor knew from past experience that this was easier said than done. Instead of engaging Judas in battle, therefore, he entered into a peace compact with the Jews, which seemed honorable and satisfactory to both sides. This did not suit the policy of Alcimus, and he boldly accused Nicanor to the king, who sent instructions that the original plans or orders must be carried out. Upon this Nicanor, much against his own judgment, advanced upon the army of Judas, who had been apprized of the violation of the compact in time to be prepared for war. At Beth-horon and Adasa the opposing hosts encamped, and, joining battle, Judas was again triumphant, and the king's soldiers beat an ignominious retreat. Nicanor was killed, and his head and right hand were carried to Jerusalem in triumph. "For this cause," says the author of 1 Maccabees (chap. 7:48–50), "the people rejoiced greatly, and they kept that day a day of great gladness. Moreover they ordained to keep yearly this day, being the thirteenth of Adar. Thus the land of Judea was in rest a little while."

But it was evident to Judas that the era of quiet could not last long, for the Syrian king would not be likely to allow this dishonor to his army to pass unavenged. The stern old warrior, Judas, therefore, determined to make an alliance with Rome, which was now the dominant power of the West, and already making her influence felt in the East. Had Judas read and understood the words of Daniel as to the rise of the fourth empire, and realized that the third was doomed? It can scarcely be doubted. He knew, too, how potent had been the word of a Roman senator in the days of Epiphanes; so it was natural enough that he should seek an alliance with the "beast dreadful and terrible, having great iron teeth." Better be a friend than a foe of such a power, he may have thought. Yet it is evident that Judas had dropped to a lower level than he had occupied in days gone by when his reliance had been alone upon the God of Israel. Rome was but an arm of flesh, and the Jews were to find in her an oppressor beyond all others ere the fruit of this pact had fully been gathered.

Negotiations were entered into with the Roman senate, and a treaty drawn up and signed, which seemed likely to ensure peace to Israel. But Judas was not to live to see it, nor indeed did the wished-for peace prove as lasting as he had hoped. Before Demetrius could be notified of the alliance with Rome and warned to beware of harming or acting unjustly toward her "friends and confederates the Jews," the energetic Syrian monarch had dispatched a force of 22,000 men against Judas, led by Bacchides and the infamous high-priest Alcimus. The army of patriots numbered but 3000. The old spirit of confidence in God seemed to be gone. Judas was anxious and troubled; his men were in fear, and urged a retreat. The worthy old warrior could not consent to this, and, because of his stern refusal, his force was farther reduced by numerous desertions. Yet he led the forlorn hope when the Syrians came upon him, and fought bravely and doggedly to the last; but ere the battle ended the hero of Israel was no more. Judas, "the hammer of God," was overwhelmed and slain!

What his death meant to the Jews, words fail to express. They were broken-hearted and in despair; though God had not left them without a leader, for his brother Jonathan at once took his place as captain-general of the little army. This was in the year 161 B.C.

The troubles of the Jews were multiplied. The "Syrian party," headed by Alcimus, endeavored with all its power to defeat the Roman alliance and re-establish the Syrians way; and for a time there was distress and civil war. But the wretched Alcimus died the next year (160 B.C), and a measure of quiet was restored. But there were other distresses; a great famine brought fearful suffering to many, and the activity of Bacchides kept Jonathan's little army continually on the defensive until, withdrawing to the wilderness of Tekoa, he managed to wear out by guerilla tactics the trained soldiers of his opponent who sought again and again to capture him, only to be repulsed and outwitted each time.

For two years there was comparative quiet; then in 158 B.C. Bacchides came again into Judea to seek the destruction of Jonathan. He was defeated, however, and favorable terms of peace concluded between the two armies.

Troubles in Syria, in connection with the claims of a pretender to the throne named Balas, caused king Demetrius to desist from further efforts to subjugate the Jews, and for several years there was quiet in Judea, while both Demetrius and Balas sought the favor and support of Jonathan and his army. In vain Demetrius offered him privilege after privilege; Jonathan could not or would not trust him. Balas, who took the name of Alexander, offered to confer the high-priesthood upon him if Jonathan would espouse his cause. After months of negotiations his offer was accepted, and at the Feast of Tabernacles, 153 B.C., Jonathan was solemnly robed in the high-priestly garments, which he assumed for the good of his people. Yet it is clear that all this was opposed to the plain word of God. Trusting to or acting in the flesh to procure a desirable end, can never be of the Holy Spirit.

When Alexander Balas and Demetrius met, the latter was defeated and slain while in retreat. Thus was Alexander confirmed as king of Syria, and to strengthen himself he entered into an alliance with the king of Egypt, who gave him his daughter as wife. Balas professed to be the natural son of Antiochus Epiphanes, and, because it served their purpose, he got the Romans to own his claim.

It seemed now as though all must be well with the Jews: a Maccabean was high-priest; the foreign party was crushed; a Roman puppet was on the Syrian throne; and a Roman-Jewish alliance was in force. What more could be needed to secure peace and prosperity? Alas, that which was most important of all now seemed to be lacking—simple trust in the living God!

The future was to prove that "vain is the help of man," and that no human arrangements can stand, or procure the end in view, if they be opposed to the word of the Lord, and spring from expediency in place of faith.

In 148 B.C. trouble again loomed large on the horizon of the Jews. The son of Demetrius, afterwards known as Nicator (the Conqueror), who had been in hiding since his father's death, determined to regain the throne and kingdom. This prince first attacked Jonathan as a supporter of the usurper Balas, but was defeated, though not until Ptolemy, the king of Egypt, had come into Palestine with an army to assist Alexander, his son-in-law. While engaged in thus helping the Jews, he learned of a plot against his own life, laid by one of Alexander's officers. Ptolemy demanded that the offender be delivered up to him. Upon Alexander's refusal, he justly concluded that the upstart-king had sanctioned the attempt to destroy him. This caused him to demand the return of his daughter and the severance of the Syro-Egyptian alliance. Ptolemy now espoused the cause of Demetrius against Alexander, and the wife of the latter was given to Demetrius, his rival.

Alexander was soon defeated and slain. His head was sent to Ptolemy, who, however, only lived three days after receiving it. In 146 B.C. Demetrius was proclaimed king of Syria and hailed as "Nicator." A rather flimsy compact existed for a time between this prince and

Jonathan, but when in 144 B.C. Antiochus, the son of Balas, arose to contest the crown with Demetrius Nicator, Jonathan severed all relations with the latter, and threw his influence on the side of Antiochus, who confirmed his right to the high-priesthood and sent him a present of golden vessels for use in the temple; also giving him permission to be clothed in purple and to wear a golden buckle, only worn by those of royal blood.

Jonathan proved an able ally. He led his army in person against Demetrius, defeating his forces; and renewing the alliance with Rome, cast all his influence on the side of the son of Balas, who was triumphantly hailed king of Syria and Palestine. He was an able and generous prince and a real friend of the Jews, who appreciated fully the part Jonathan had taken in aiding his cause; but he was destined to reign for a very short season, falling a victim to the treachery of Tryphon, one who was largely instrumental in placing him upon the throne. Ere Antiochus fell, Jonathan was also fated to die by the machinations of the same traitorous commander.

Tryphon coveted the crown for himself, and realizing that the son of Mattathias was as a bulwark of the throne, he craftily sought to obtain possession of his person. Under a pretence of inviting him for friendly conference, Jonathan was prevailed upon to enter the city of Ptolemais, accompanied by less than a thousand men. These troops were cruelly massacred and their leader imprisoned. Upon this news reaching the surrounding nations, they prepared to invade Judea now that the veteran leader was powerless to aid his people. Tryphon also set out at the head of an army to overrun the land, determined to subjugate the "eternal" nation. Fear filled the souls of the men of Israel, and they were in despair until Simon, the brother of Jonathan, came to the front, encouraged their hearts by recounting the deeds of valor performed of old, and was unanimously chosen as captain of the host.

Hearing this, Tryphon notified Simon that Jonathan had been apprehended and imprisoned because of his failure to pay the tribute-money, and that if he, Simon, would send two hundred talents of silver and two sons of the high-priest and commander as hostages, their father would be released. Simon had little faith in the traitor's promises, but he thought it best to comply, hoping thereby to save his brother's life. All was of no avail, however; for after receiving the money and securing the hostages, Tryphon had Jonathan brutally murdered, and resumed operations against the Jews. This was in 144 B.C.—seventeen years after Jonathan had become the leader of his people. His body was later recovered, and buried at Modin, his former home.

Tryphon shortly afterwards secretly slew the youthful king Antiochus and laid hands on the crown, declaring himself king. He was a relentless enemy of the Jews, and during his troublous reign caused them much discomfort.

Demetrius Nicator, the deposed king, who had been driven out by the armies of Antiochus, was still alive and plotting to regain the royal dignity. It seemed to Simon that he was much to be preferred to the detestable Tryphon, so he decided to espouse his cause. Sending him a crown of gold and a robe of scarlet, Simon sought to make a treaty with him which would insure peace between them. This greatly pleased Demetrius, who readily agreed and confirmed the high-priesthood to

Simon, forgave the Jews all tribute, and declared all past faults forgiven. He really surrendered his title to Palestine as a whole, so that Simon was virtually governor of a free people, if able to hold their own against Tryphon. Thus the Syrian servitude of 170 years came to an end in that year, 143 B.C. At the same time the Romans confirmed their former league on plates of brass, and the Lacedemonians also entered into a peaceful alliance with Israel, so that Tryphon dared no longer molest them.

For a brief period the land enjoyed rest and prosperity under the wise leadership of Simon. The cities were rebuilt, the lands tilled, and the arts of peace pursued. So pleased were the people of the Jews with Simon, that they held a general assembly in his third year, 141 B.C., when they conferred the priesthood and the government upon him and his heirs forever, engraving their decision in brass and fixing it upon pillars in Mount Zion.

But again misfortune loomed darkly on the horizon; for in the same year they became involved once more in the quarrels of the rival claimants to the Syrian throne. Demetrius Nicator had been captured by the king of Persia, and his brother Antiochus Pius usurped the kingly title and prepared to contest his claim with Tryphon. Obtaining permission from Simon to pass through his lands in order to recover the territories ruled over by his father, he led an army against Tryphon, whom he defeated, thus obtaining the dominion he sought. Though he had confirmed all the pledges given by his brother to Simon, he became jealous of the latter's power and liberty, and sent an army to invade Judea, with orders to seize the government and carry captive all who opposed his authority.

Simon, though very old, roused himself to the defence of his people in true Maccabean spirit, and putting his sons Judas and John (known as Hyrcanus) in command of the army, met the foe in bloody conflict and defeated him, to the great elation of the Jews. But their joy was turned into mourning when very soon afterwards Simon and two of his sons were assassinated at a banquet, and that through the treachery of his son-in-law, named Ptolemy. Thus died the last of the famous sons of the stern old God-fearing patriot Mattathias, in 135 B.C.

RUINS OF ANTONIA, THE PALACE OF THE MACCABEES
(JERUSALEM)

For us, who are seeking to learn lessons of practical value from all this, one thing stands out as a solemn warning: the people of the Jews had largely lost that godly separation and dependence which should have been their sanctification. In their distresses, in place of implicit reliance on the God of their fathers, they turned to alliances with the heathen, depending on an arm of flesh that often failed them, and was to be their ruin in the end. Who that is even ordinarily familiar with the history of the Church, can fail to see that the same snare has ever been the bane of every movement which in its early beginnings was marked by devotedness to Christ and reliance upon the living God, but which as the freshness of early days passed away, and numbers were added who had obtained the truth at little cost (often coming into it almost by natural birth), lost this peculiar link with the Divine, and depended more and more on what was merely human? This is the weakness of practically every religious society, and no company of Christians can afford to be indifferent to the danger of such a course. Power and blessing, victory and spiritual freshness are the portion of those who cleave to the Lord alone. Weakness and barrenness as surely follow upon amalgamation with the world, as in the case of the Jews in the days upon which we have been dwelling.

III. To the End of the Asmonean Dynasty

JOHN HYRCANUS, son of Simon, succeeded to the place and honor of his father, in accordance with the decision of the great council. His first act was to attempt the relief of his mother, who was held captive by her unworthy son-in-law Ptolemy. In this he was unsuccessful. The aged woman was murdered, and her assassin could not be apprehended. Antiochus Pius again invaded the land, determined if possible to crush the independent spirit of the Jews, but he was once more outwitted, though the cause of much suffering for weary months. At the feast of tabernacles of that year a treaty was signed which rather gave the advantage to the Syrians, and Antiochus returned to his own land, after having sent a costly sacrifice to the temple at Jerusalem as a sop to Jewish pride.

Antiochus did not hold his sceptre long, for in the year 130 B.C. he fell in battle with the Parthians, and his ill-starred brother, Demetrius, came out of captivity to succeed him, reigning a little over four years, and being himself slain, 126 B.C.

John Hyrcanus renewed the league with the Romans, in order to strengthen himself against the Syrians, whom he attacked in several cities with varying loss and gain; in the main successful, however. He introduced a new policy (too often followed since, alas, even by what professes to be the Church), namely, compelling the conquered peoples to abjure their systems of worship and conform to Judaism by becoming circumcised, and thus be added to the Jewish people, or giving them the alternative of a violent death. But forcible proselyting could only result in disaster. Converts by coercion were ever an element of weakness.

It must be evident to the most cursory reader that the Jews had allowed themselves to greatly decline from the spirituality of the days of Ezra and Nehemiah, or even the zeal for the covenant of the days of Judas Maccabeus. Formality and rationalism were eating the very life out of them. They gloried in their past history, but were far from present subjection to the law of God. Thus has it ever been when the twin evils of either narrow party spirit or broad latitudinarianism have been allowed to do their deadly and soul-destroying work. The one makes bigoted fanatics, who imagine that all divine counsels centre in themselves, and become intolerant, formal and exacting. The other produces careless, pleasure-loving "broad-churchmanlike" professors, who are indifferent to all that is vital in religion, content to have a form of godliness while denying its power.

Such were the opposite characteristics of the two great parties that for years had been forming among the Jews, and which had in the times of Hyrcanus become definitely separated and designated as the sects of the "Pharisees" and "Sadducees." The Maccabees were ever of the former company, until now, when John Hyrcanus made it manifest that he had decided leanings towards the more liberal Sadducees. For a time he remained nominally a Pharisee, until at a certain feast, a leader of the "most straitest sect" demanded of him that he resign the priesthood, which had been held by the Asmoneans since Jonathan, in plain disobedience to the letter of the law. Hyrcanus indignantly inquired the reason for this request; and the one who had made it, not daring to be frank, said it was because it had been bruited abroad that the mother of the high-priest was a Gentile, one who had been taken captive in the war. This story, palpably false, enraged Hyrcanus, who demanded that the calumniator be severely punished. The latter was declared to be guilty of an offence punishable only by bonds and stripes. The lightness of the sentence seemed to convince Hyrcanus that the Pharisees really upheld the man, and he ended the matter by turning away from them altogether and openly joining the Sadducean faction. Edersheim very properly designates this act as "the beginning of the decline of the Maccabees." Henceforth they sank by quick changes to the level of the company they kept.

Hyrcanus rapidly lost his influence with the mass of the people, and being both secretly and openly opposed by the Pharisees, his after years were full of trouble and distress. In 107 B.C. he died, having accomplished little that could be said to be to God's praise or the blessing of the Jews, though Josephus (evidently a partial critic) says he possessed the gift of prophecy. He appointed his wife to be "mistress of all" after his death; but she was set aside by her son Aristobulus, who succeeded to the dignities and authority of his father. This man added nothing to the decaying glory of the family, though he was the first of his race to assume the title of king of the Jews—a title which Zerubbabel, of the royal family of David, would not take in the days of the restoration.

The young king left a brief but blood-stained record behind him. He became the murderer of his mother—imprisoning and starving her to death, and slew or imprisoned all his brothers. Within a year he had gone the way of all flesh, dying in 106 B.C.

His widow, Salome, then released his living brethren, and made the eldest king. He was known as Alexander Janneus. The Greek names of these sons of Hyrcanus show how far from the Maccabean spirit their degenerate children had drifted. Alexander slew one of his brothers, permitting the other to live, and occupied himself in wars of conquest; his sister-in-law, Salome, acting as regent of the kingdom during his campaigns.

The Pharisees were still the dominant party in Jerusalem, while the king was openly a Sadducee. He detested the strictness of the separatists and publicly defied them on one memorable occasion by pouring the water from the Pool of Siloam upon the ground instead of the altar, at the feast of tabernacles. This was a ceremony prescribed, not in the law, but the ritual, and referred to by our Lord in John 7:37, 38. A terrible uproar was precipitated by what the Pharisees regarded as a sacrilegious act, and Alexander called in his foreign troops to quell the riot. So fearful was the disturbance, that ere it was put down six thousand people had been slain. But this was only the beginning. Rebellion and insurrection broke out everywhere, and before peace was established some fifty thousand persons were killed. In their desperation, the Pharisees and their followers intrigued with their ancient foes, the Syrians, who sent an army to help them, hoping thereby to recover Palestine for themselves. At their first battle Alexander was defeated, and the victorious foreigners began to overrun the land. This changed matters somewhat; it caused many who previously had either opposed or been noncommittal, to rally to the standard of Alexander. His army was so strengthened that the Syrians felt it would be hopeless in the then state of the inflamed populace to pursue their plans; so they withdrew. In the party strife that followed, Alexander carried all before him, and crushed out the last spark of insurrection in a most barbarous manner, following the heathen custom of crucifying and mutilating vast numbers of men, women and even children, thus rendering his throne secure and his name infamous! His cruelty won for him the title of "the Thracian."

His reign was somewhat lengthy (twenty-seven years), and in his later years he vigorously carried on his policy of subjugating and proselytizing by force the surrounding nations, who were given the alternative of submitting to circumcision or being put to death. He died in 79 B.C., and in his will directed that his body be given to his old opponents the Pharisees to do with it as they would. This unexpected submission of the grim warrior so surprised and pleased them that they buried him in great honor.

It was during his reign, about 88 B.C., as pointed out by Prideaux, that Phanuel, the husband of Anna the prophetess, died, according to Luke 2:36, 37, for she had been "a widow of about fourscore and four years" at the time of the presentation of the infant Jesus in the temple. Allowing for the difference of four years between B.C. and A. D., this would place her husband's death as mentioned. Thus we come now to the first link with the New Testament. Anna was a wife and a widow in the reign of Alexander; through all the turbulent years that followed, she ever waited for the consolation of Israel, and she was in the temple to welcome the promised Messiah when His mother and His foster father first brought Him up to the house of God to carry out the legal ritual regarding the birth of a male child. Simeon's age is not given, but he too may have been living ere Alexander Janneus died, or else he must have been born shortly afterward.

Two sons were left by "the Thracian," named Hyrcanus and Aristobulus; but he directed in his will that his wife Alexandra should succeed him; and as the Jews generally regarded her as opposed to the policies of her late husband, the nation concurred in his choice. She was accordingly acknowledged as queen-regent, though Josephus declares, "the Pharisees had the authority." She appointed her son Hyrcanus high-priest, but he was a weak, vacillating man, who had little interest either in matters of religion or affairs of state, and readily acquiesced in the will of the dominant party. The Pharisees repealed the decrees of John Hyrcanus and "bound" and "loosed" whom they would. So active and offensive were they that many who would not conform to their wishes fled from Jerusalem, or obtained leave from the queen to settle elsewhere, as it was impossible for them to live in peace in the capital unless they accepted the dogmas and followed the usages of these extreme legalists, who then dominated the state.

These non-conformists, on the other hand, were as far removed from subjection to the law of God as to the traditions of the elders. They were of the Sadducean caste—loose in their lives, liberal in their religious views, and Gentilizers in politics. They entrenched themselves in fortresses at various points, and secretly plotted the downfall of their enemies, the Pharisees.

Aristobulus, the brother of Hyrcanus, sympathized with these men. He despised his indolent brother, hated the stern, puritanical principles of the Pharisees and coveted the crown and kingdom. But he bided his time, until at last a serious illness attacked the queen. Upon learning this, he hastened from Jerusalem and rallying the exiles, soon had some twenty-two strongholds and a very respectable army at his command. Too late, Hyrcanus realized the folly of inaction, and urgently sought to have the queen proclaim him the heir; but she died before anything could be done.

Thus the two brothers found themselves at the head of rival factions. Hyrcanus led out an army to meet Aristobulus and his troops, but no battle was fought, for most of the high-priest's soldiers deserted to his younger brother, and Hyrcanus fled in terror to Jerusalem. Finally, terms of peace were arranged whereby Aristobulus was proclaimed king and Hyrcanus confirmed in the priesthood.

Each seemed satisfied with this arrangement, and peace might have been maintained for years had it not been for the ambition and machinations of a man of whom we have not hitherto spoken, but who was destined to play a large part in Jewish history for years to come.

This man was an Idumean, named Antipater. He was the father of Herod the Great who, by a strange combination of circumstances, was to be "the king of the Jews," in whose reign the long-expected Messiah was to be born.

Antipater was not a Jew, but of the hated Edomite race, the descendants of Esau, though a proselyte, outwardly at least, of Judaism. Under king Alexander he had been appointed governor of Idumea, and had become possessed of great power and authority. He was retained in that position by Queen Alexandra. Hyrcanus and Antipater were close friends, and the latter was not at all pleased to see the regal authority given to the younger brother. He evidently feared his own aspirations might be blighted by the downfall of the high-priest. So he determined to act at once, and act vigorously, to thwart this. Persuading Hyrcanus that his life was in danger through the plotting of Aristobulus, he finally prevailed upon the easy-going priest to flee to Aretas, king of Arabia, who was also in the plot and one of Antipater's friends. An arrangement was made whereby the three allies, Hyrcanus, Aretas and Antipater raised an army of 50,000 men, with which they set out to overthrow Aristobulus. "Biting and devouring one another," the Jews were in grave danger of "being consumed one of another"—a lesson to all religious controversialists since!

The king of Judea, utterly unable to cope with such a host, dared not give battle, but fled to Jerusalem and shut himself up there for safety. He was besieged by the Arabians and the discontented Jews, who both by might and trickery sought to have him delivered up by the people. The mass were in favor of Hyrcanus, but the priests, who were largely of the Sadducees, generally sided with Aristobulus. Their influence was strong enough to keep the populace from opening the gates to the besiegers, and so the investment of the city dragged on for weary weeks and months.

Among the priests was an eccentric character of some influence and piety, named Onias, who was declared to be a remarkable man of prayer. It was told of him that on one occasion, during a season of prolonged drought, causing great suffering and distress, he had drawn a circle round himself with his rod in the sand, and declared that he would never cross over it until his prayers were heard and rain was given. How long he remained thus enclosed we do not know, but he did not move out of the self-imposed limits until the welcome showers began to fall. The enthusiastic people called him ever after *Onias Ham-meaggel:* that is, *Circle-drawer Onias*. In some way this man fell into the hands of the besieging forces, who took him to their camp and commanded him to pray for the success of the cause of Hyrcanus and against Aristobulus and the priestly Sadducean faction. The Jews in the beleaguering army were insistent, and would brook no refusal. After pleading in vain for liberty, Onias at last arose and prayed: "O God, King of the whole world, since those who stand with me now are Thy people, and those who are besieged are Thy priests, I pray Thee harken Thou neither to the entreaty of those against these, nor bring to effect what these pray against those." The multitude rushed upon him in a rage, and he was mercilessly stoned to death. The incident shows the prevailing temper and affords a melancholy view of the condition of mind in which the people were found at the time. A passionate, factional spirit was withering up all piety, save in "the poor of the flock" who waited for the shining forth of the Sun of righteousness.

As the siege dragged on, it came near the sacred passover season, and there were no beasts in the city for the sacrifices. This obliged the priests to come to some terms with the besiegers, and the latter agreed to supply cattle and sheep at the exorbitant price of a thousand drachmas for each beast. The money was gathered, and passed over the walls to those appointed to receive it, but no beasts were given in return, and the priests were in despair.

Relief at last came in an unlooked-for way. Pompey, the noted Roman general, sent forces under Scaurus and

Gabinius into Syria to restore order there. Each section of the Jews sent emissaries to Damascus to seek the aid of the Romans against the others, and at last through bribery the party of Aristobulus won, and at command of the Romans the allies retreated and were pursued and utterly routed by the priestly party. As a reward for timely aid, the Jews presented a golden crown to Pompey who had come to Damascus.

But the troubles of the Jews were far from a settlement. Antipater determined to carry his cause in person to Pompey, and was graciously heard by the latter. Aristobulus then determined to do the same, but offended by his rude, insolent bearing. A third party also appeared, and declared that both Hyrcanus and his brother were unauthorized upstarts and disturbers of the commonwealth, and the people asked that both be set aside and other rulers appointed in their places. Aristobulus feared his was a losing cause, and hastily leaving Damascus, fled to Alexandrium, where Pompey pursued him. Allowing the town, which was a fortress, to fall into the general's hands, the king fell back and retreated to Jerusalem, which he sought to put in condition to stand another siege. Upon the appearance of Pompey before the walls, however, Aristobulus changed his mind, offered to surrender and to pay any required indemnity. To this Pompey agreed; and holding Aristobulus as a hostage, sent an agent into the city to collect the promised money.

But the Jewish soldiers were not disposed thus tamely to accede to the demands of the Romans; the deputation found the city guarded and the walls manned for defence, while the request for indemnity was refused. All in the city were not agreed as to the policy of the soldiers, but they carried the day, and the siege was renewed.

Eventually the lower part of the city surrendered, and the Temple Hill alone held out, despite the efforts of the invaders to take it by assault and casting military mounds, from which missiles of various kinds were projected into the fortress. Learning by experience that the Jews refrained from all offensive tactics on the Sabbath, the Romans did the same, and spent each seventh day strengthening their earth-works and putting themselves in a better position to storm the walls. In this way a decided advantage was gained, but nevertheless the desperate little band of zealots held out for over three months. Finally, a Roman battering-ram demolished one of the largest towers; through the breach thus made, the besiegers pressed their way, and a fearful scene of carnage followed.

It is said that twelve thousand persons perished by sword and fire on that fearful day, the horrors of which no pen could describe, and indeed it would be but soul-harrowing to attempt it. Many of the priests were cut down in the temple itself as they officiated in holy things; for through all the siege and final fall of the city the service had been kept up, while the cries of the distracted people were in vain addressed to God who, in accordance with the prophecy of Hosea, given some centuries earlier but still unrepealed, had cast them off as not His people. Individuals indeed were owned and saved, but the nation as such He would not own, and in deepest woe they reaped the bitter fruit of years of evil sowing.

This was the end of Jewish independence. Henceforth Judea was but a Roman province. How little had

Judas Maccabeus foreseen what the result of his treaty with Rome would mean to his people! Better far would it have been to have depended alone upon the Lord of Hosts than to have placed confidence in Rome.

Pompey deprived Hyrcanus of all kingly honors, but confirmed him in the high-priesthood and ordered the temple service continued. He had polluted the holy place by entering it himself, but afterwards gave orders for its purification, thus pacifying the Jews. Aristobulus he carried as a captive to Rome, together with his son Antigonus; another son, Alexander, was also a prisoner, but escaped before reaching the Imperial City. He afterwards made a futile attempt to revive the Jewish state, but Gabinius, the Roman general, left in charge by Pompey, defeated him in 57 B.C. A little later Aristobulus escaped, and making his way to Palestine, endeavored to stir up revolt, but in vain. He was re-captured and returned to Rome in chains. In 55 B.C. Alexander tried once more, but could get no following of any moment, and was defeated at Mount Tabor.

Gabinius governed Judea under Scaurus, who was appointed over all the region once ruled by the Seleucidæ. He restored order in the desolated land, established a firm and able government, respected the rights of the Jews so far as was compatible with Roman policy, and really gave far more satisfaction than had the degenerate sons of the Maccabees. Hyrcanus submitted peaceably to the yoke and was befriended by Antipater who, on his part, had the confidence and good-will of Pompey.

Thus for a season a measure of prosperity succeeded the hard and difficult years that had been the lot of the

Jews for so long. The next year it was rudely disturbed by a visit from Crassus who was now consul in conjunction with Pompey in Rome. Being in need of money, Crassus marched to Jerusalem determined to lay hands on the temple treasure, the vast extent of which had aroused his cupidity. In vain Eleazar, the priest in charge, sought to divert him from his impious purpose by offering instead a large ingot of gold which had been hidden away. Crassus took the gold and the treasure also, and carried away to Rome a quantity of money, jewels and plate, estimated at some ten millions of dollars.

This so aroused the Jews, that many rallied about Alexander, and he, for the third time, raised the standard for revolt. Crassus returned in 52 B.C. and forced him to terms of peace. Two years later Scipio was made president of Syria, and in Rome Cæsar and Pompey were at strife. In order to gain an advantage over Pompey, Julius Caesar liberated Aristobulus and aided him to return to Judea, with two legions of soldiers. His son Alexander was to raise a force and join his father. But Scipio, as a friend of Pompey, nipped the plot in the bud by apprehending and beheading Alexander, while other agents of Pompey contrived to poison Aristobulus ere he reached Judea.

JERUSALEM FROM THE MOUNT OF OLIVES

Thus Antigonus alone remained of the sons of Aristobulus. Of him and his unfortunate end we shall hear later. He never regained the crown save for a very short time, though he fought desperately for it. The Asmonean princes by their profligacy and godlessness had lost all that their noble fathers had gained.

The glory had departed and Shiloh had not yet come! Was the word of God to be discredited at last, and the hope of Israel go out in darkness? Not so; the tribal sceptre should not depart from Judah till Messiah appeared, though it was preserved in such a way as "to hide pride from man" and to give exercise for faith. God would preserve a light in Jerusalem and maintain His people in their land till *He* should come whose advent had so long been foretold, but it should be under the fostering care of the hated Edomite, whose object should be but his own glory and exaltation.

IV. THE EDOMITE ASCENDANCY

WE closed our last chapter with Hyrcanus still occupying the office of high-priest, under the patronage, though really the authority, of Antipater, and both subject to Scipio. Antigonus alone remained of the adult Asmonean princes, and he was still in captivity. We now hasten on to the events of the last half century ere the birth of our Lord Jesus Christ.

Pompey's star set as that of Julius Cæsar dominated the firmament. The latter came into Syria in 47 B.C., and made a relative, Sextus Cæsar, president of the province. Returning shortly to Rome, he was made Dictator of the world.

Antipater had been able to ingratiate himself with Cæsar in his expedition against the Pontians and Cappadocians, and in return the Dictator made him a free citizen of Rome, and constituted him Procurator of Judea. Thus had the crafty Edomite reached the position for which he had long been scheming. He remained the friend and patron of Hyrcanus, and supported him against the appeals of Antigonus, who was endeavoring to win the favor of Cæsar. But the Procurator was no longer a young man. His honors had been late in coming, and he found the additional burdens heavy to bear. Accordingly he appointed his two sons, Phasael and Herod, governors of Galilee and of Jerusalem respectively, thus putting the Holy Land fully under Idumean rule. On the other hand, it should not be forgotten that Idumea had been conquered by John Hyrcanus, 130 B.C., and the nation forcibly converted and circumcised, so that Antipater and his descendants, though of the house of Esau, were now Jews in religion, at least outwardly. And the after-history of the family shows that they valued Judaism from a *religio-politico* standpoint; their constant efforts being in opposition to the Grecianizing policy of some of the Jewish rulers. The glory of their race they conceived to be bound up with the triumph of the ancient ritual. It was Esau's last and fruitless effort to obtain the blessing of Jacob, forfeited so long before.

Herod was but a youth of twenty years (or, as some say, only fifteen), when appointed by his father to the governorship of Judea. He was a young man of extraordinary energy and ability, and in his earlier years, before lust and ambition had done their deadly work, was characterized by many attractive qualities. But he made what might have been a fatal mistake very soon after assuming the dignities of his office. In Galilee an uprising took place of Jewish zealots, whom Josephus (out of deference to the foreigners upon whom he fawned) calls "a horde of robbers." Herod suppressed this incipient rebellion, and, without the consent of the Sanhedrim, put their leader to death. For this act of rashness he was summoned to answer before the great council, jealous of his Idumean descent and of their own prerogatives.

Hyrcanus trembled for the outcome. He was a friend of Herod, and yet did not wish to appear to take sides against the council. Sextus Cæsar wrote commanding him to clear the young governor, who had but acted as a faithful servant of Rome. Could he have done so decently, Hyrcanus would have rescinded the order of the Sanhedrim, but that was impossible under the circumstances, so Herod was called to account. He appeared, robed in royal purple, accompanied by an armed guard, and with all the bearing of a great official rather than a person on trial for a grave offence. His manner overawed the Jewish priests and doctors, who were about to acquit him, when the aged president of the council, Sameas, spoke out boldly for condemnation, declaring with what seemed like the voice of prophecy that, if they freed him, "this man whom they sought to absolve, would one day punish them all." Stirred by the old man's fiery words, the judges decided to pronounce sentence of death. Hyrcanus, upon learning their intention, suddenly prorogued the council, and sent word to Herod secretly to flee for his life, acquainting him with the mind of the elders.

The governor at once withdrew from the city; but in place of recognizing his indebtedness to the high-priest, came against him with an army, determined to destroy him as the representative of the system that had dared to question his authority. Antipater got word of his movements in time to interfere, and Herod was dissuaded from his purpose. He afterwards had his revenge by slaying the entire Sanhedrim, with the exception of a man named Pollio, and the aged Sameas who had counselled his death.

For several years the walls of Jerusalem had been left in a state of ruin, ever since Pompey's triumphal entry, until in 44 B.C. Julius Cæsar authorized Antipater and Hyrcanus to repair them. The work was begun at once, though greatly hindered by the kaleidoscopic events of the next few years. Cæsar was slain by Brutus and his co-conspirators a few months after issuing the order to rebuild the walls, and for some time confusion reigned not only in Rome but in the various provinces. In Judea Antipater had difficulty in maintaining his authority, and was eventually poisoned by an agent of the anarchistic element by the name of Malichus, who in turn was done to death by one of Herod's agents after considerable disputations and unrest.

The friends of Malichus claimed Hyrcanus as one of their party, but this seems unlikely. The old man's vacillating character made him the plaything of the whirling eddies in the political stream, and subjected him to much misunderstanding and misrepresentation. Herod, however, seems to have believed the high-priest was in the plot, but took no extreme steps; chiefly, perhaps, because he was espoused to the grand-daughter of Hyrcanus, Mariamne, of bitter memory.

In 42 B.C., Antigonus, of whom little had been heard for some years, again appeared and, raising an army of malcontents, made another effort to secure the crown. Herod acted with his accustomed energy and easily defeated him, driving him into exile. Antigonus appealed to Mark Antony, the Roman general and friend of the slain Cæsar, but without success; for Herod had been beforehand in the matter and had won Antony's regard by large sums of money. Antony appointed Phasael tetrarch of Galilee and Herod tetrarch of Judea, thus raising their rank and confirming their authority.

The desperate Antigonus next fled to Parthia and made a league with the king of that country, who furnished him with an army for the payment of one thousand talents and five hundred Jewish women! How low had a prince of the Maccabean line fallen who could thus sell his country-women into a slavery far worse than death! By acting quickly Antigonus took Jerusalem by assault, imprisoned Phasael and Hyrcanus, and would have apprehended Herod himself, had not the latter fled in the night with a few relatives and friends who preferred to risk misfortunes with him rather than be exposed to the wrath of Antigonus. Supported by the Parthians, Antigonus was declared king, and set up a puppet court. In order that Hyrcanus might never again be high-priest, the wretched prince bit off his ears, thus maiming the aged prelate and rendering him, according to Levitical law, unfit to serve in the temple. He then gave him into the hands of the Parthians, who took him away to their own country. Hyrcanus was afterwards slain by Herod, when he regained his authority.

Phasael, the brother of Herod, remained in prison, until feeling that his death was decreed by Antigonus and the Parthians, he decided to slay himself rather than die by their hands; so he dashed his brains out against the stone walls of his cell.

Herod sought shelter in Arabia, but it was refused him; upon which he made his way to Egypt, and there took ship for Rome, which he reached in safety, after being very nearly shipwrecked in a tempest. He repaired to the presence of Antony, who received him with much favor, listened with sympathy to his pitiful story, and commended him to Octavius Cæsar and the senate. The latter conferred upon him the title of king of Judea, and sent him back to Palestine with full authority to dispossess the usurper and maintain his own title by force of arms. In seven days after Herod's arrival in Rome as a fugitive with a price on his head, he sailed for Judea with a band of soldiers hailing him as king. This was in 40 B.C.

Herod landed at Ptolemais, and learning that his mother, sister, and Mariamne, his betrothed, were shut up in Masada, where they were besieged by Antigonus, he put himself at the head of the Roman legions, marched rapidly to the battle-ground, raised the siege, and placed his relatives in safety. He then moved quickly on from place to place, defeated the nationalist bands at every turn, and pushed on to Jerusalem, which he besieged for two years. It fell in 37 B.C., through the aid of Sosius, the president of Syria, whose soldiers were guilty of such atrocities that even the cruel Herod had to beg Sosius to restrain them, lest he be but king of a desert! It was at this time that all of the Sanhedrim but two were slain. Antigonus pleaded for mercy, but Sosius treated him with scorn and contempt, calling him "Antigone" (the feminine form of his name), and sending him in chains to Antony at Rome. Herod bribed the latter to destroy him, and he was beheaded as a rebel against the empire.

A year before, Herod had been married to the beautiful but ill-fated Mariamne, through which alliance he hoped to win the favor of the Jews, as his queen was of the Asmonean line; but in this he was unsuccessful, for his cruelty made him hated by all. "Better be Herod's pig than Herod's son" was a proverb in after years.

There remained yet one male descendant of the Maccabees, a young man named Aristobulus, Mariamne's brother. This young Asmonean was the hope of such as still dared to look forward to the re-establishment of the Jewish line. He was the son of Alexandra, daughter of Hyrcanus, and of Alexander, son of Aristobulus, Hyrcanus' brother; he was therefore of unquestioned Maccabean blood. Alexandra sought to have him appointed high-priest, but Herod passed him over in favor of an obscure priest from Babylon, on whom he thought he could depend to carry out his will in any emergency that might arise. Alexandra was greatly angered by this, and applied to Cleopatra, the Egyptian queen, for aid, beseeching her to use her influence with Antony in her son's behalf. She was successful. Herod was overruled, and Aristobulus made high-priest. At the feast of tabernacles he appeared before the people, a handsome youth, clad in the gorgeous robes of the pontiff of Israel. As they thus beheld an Asmonean again officiating in the solemn rites, the joy of the Jews was great, and they applauded rapturously. Their acclamations stirred Herod's jealousy, and immediately after the celebration the high-priest was "accidentally" drowned in the king's fish-ponds at Jericho.

Herod appeared to be pained and surprised at the untimely end of the last male scion of the Maccabees, and gave him a magnificent funeral, appearing himself as chief mourner. But all this sham and pretense failed to deceive the Jews, who knew that Aristobulus had been murdered at the king's command. Alexandra appealed to Antony for judgment against Herod, again prevailing upon Cleopatra to speak for her. Herod was cited to appear before Antony to answer for the crime charged against him. He appointed his uncle, Joseph, procurator in his absence, committed his wife Mariamne (the only person he ever loved) to his care, and obeyed at once, leaving secret instructions that in the event of his condemnation and death, she was to be assassinated immediately. Josephus tells us that Joseph let Mariamne into the secret, and ironically remarks, she "did not take this to be an instance of Herod's strong affection!"

A rumor was soon circulated in Jerusalem that Herod had been found guilty and put to death by torture; upon which Alexandra endeavored to secure the throne. She had been misled, however, for soon Herod returned, fully exonerated; his bribes having proven more powerful than Cleopatra's pleading. Herod then cast Alexandra into prison for a time, but his fury having abated, Alexandra was released from prison.

Domestic troubles now broke out in the household of Herod, hurrying him on to fearful crimes which threw their dark shadow over all the rest of his career. His sister Salome, jealous of Mariamne's influence over her brother, accused her secretly of unfaithfulness, naming Joseph as the guilty paramour. Herod pretended not to credit this, but became jealous and suspicious when Mariamne asked him how he could have given instructions to kill her if he really loved her? Convinced of his uncle's perfidy, he slew him without trial, but for the present spared his wife. In 29 B.C. he was called before Octavius, and ere he left home repeated his former order. In some way Mariamne again learned of it, and when Herod returned, bitterly reproached him for his want of confidence and affection. In his jealous fury he had her put to death, only to become shortly after the victim of fearful remorse. Despair and resentment filled his mind with gloom and horror. So terribly was he affected that he fell ill, and became deranged for a time.

While Herod was in this state, Alexandra conceived the idea of again making an effort to possess herself of the government; but her plot was discovered; Herod roused himself from his melancholy, and she was put to death for her crime (28 B.C.) Thus had the Asmonean family been obliterated and the hopes of Israel almost quenched.

Not through Mattathias, however, but through David was the Seed to come through whom all the world should be blessed. And God had still preserved the royal line, though now sunk in poverty and obscurity. The "fulness of time" had almost come when the promise at last was to be fulfilled.

Meantime the bloody Edomite sat on David's throne, and his course became more and more vile as the years went on. Mariamne had borne him two sons, Alexander and Aristobulus. These boys were sent to Rome to be educated. Upon their return, at the instigation of their vindictive aunt Salome, who had been the cause of their mother's death, *they* were strangled. Their half-brother Antipater, son of a former Idumean wife, Doris, had been named as Herod's successor in 11 B.C., and in 6 B.C. the strangulation took place. The wretched king went through a semblance of law in the matter, citing his sons before the council, and there so vehemently accusing them, that sentence of death was passed upon the unhappy youths. Shortly afterwards his son, Antipater, was accused of plotting to secure the throne at once by poisoning his father, and he also was executed by Herod's orders.

Yet through all these years of intrigues, family quarrels, and bloodshed, Herod did much for the up-building of Jerusalem and the prosperity of Palestine. He built many great cities on a plan far above anything previously attempted by the Jews. As a general, he was everywhere victorious; as a diplomat, he knew no equal; as a legislator, he displayed unexampled wisdom and care for his kingdom and the interests of his people. A lover of the arts and a patron of religion, he was, nevertheless, a monster of impiety, an Idumean Nero, who would stop at nothing to attain his selfish ends.

It was this Herod, so-called "the Great," that rebuilt the temple in unparallelled grandeur; and he made it his boast to have outdone Solomon himself. The restored building gleamed with gold and costly marbles, and was the pride of the nation of Israel and the wonder of their neighbors. Once he had set his mind upon the attainment of any object, Herod allowed nothing to hinder the consummation desired. He moved on through bloody crimes and vilest barbarities to the goal he had before him of being considered the ablest and wealthiest of the kings of the East, winning thus for himself the title "Magnus," or as we say, Herod the Great.

And now, as we draw near the close of Herod's life, we must remind the reader that our Saviour was born four years before the popular reckoning known as *Anno Domini*. When in the sixth century of the Christian era, it was determined to begin dating from the birth of our Lord, a mistake of four years was made in computing the exact time. This was only recognized many centuries later, and it would have thrown all subsequent chronology into confusion to have sought then to rectify the error. Consequently, strange as it appears to write it, Christ was born in the year 4 B.C. This was but two years after the judicial murder of the sons of Herod and Mariamne. Consequently it was in that year the angel of the Lord announced first to Zecharias the birth of a son in his old age, John, who should be the forerunner of his Lord, to prepare the way before Him; and later to Mary the fulfilment of the Promise through her, in the birth of Him who was to be called *Emmanuel*—our Lord and Saviour Jesus Christ.

It is no wonder that, upon the arrival of the wise men from the East, inquiring as to a new King of the Jews, the guilty monarch suspected a plot. He craftily inquired of the priests and scribes as to the Jewish expectations and hopes of a Messiah-King under pretense of giving Him honor; and when he saw that he was "mocked of the wise men," issued the mandate for the slaying of all the infants of Bethlehem.

Christ had indeed been born to be not only King of the Jews, but King of kings and Lord of lords. Herod and all of his class were as men doomed to destruction, whose lives were prolonged for a little season that repentance and remission of sins might be preached to all nations ere the King so long expected should fall like the mighty Stone from heaven on all the kingdoms of earth, and henceforth rule in righteousness and everlasting peace.

Herod's death occurred, as narrated in the Gospel, during the time the Infant Saviour was hidden in Egypt, and he was succeeded by Archelaus, as we also read in Matthew.

But it is not part of our task to follow the further course of events with which every reader of the New Testament is familiar. We set out to tell the story of the "Four Hundred Silent Years" which intervened between the Old and New Testaments, which God has seen fit to leave blank in our Bibles. Our task, therefore, save for a closing chapter on the literature of that period, is now done.

The reader will have little difficulty in realizing why the Saviour was not received by the covenant people. Their long years of declension had rendered them unable to recognize their Messiah when He appeared in accord with the scriptures of the Prophets. Their eyes had become blinded; their ears heavy; their hearts hardened, and their consciences seared; and so, not knowing the Scriptures, they fulfilled them in condemning the Prince of Life. Yet they were in Immanuel's land and the Holy City; gathered to the place where Jehovah's Name had been set of old. They were punctilious about the services of the temple; fond of reasoning about the Scriptures; proud of their descent from the patriarchs; and in their self-righteous complacency, despising their Gentile neighbors. But all this availed nothing when spiritual discernment was gone and religion a matter of ritual rather than of life. It is not necessary to press the lesson for our own times. He who sees it not himself would not heed it if another urged it upon him.

V. THE LITERATURE OF THE JEWS

WHEN one meditates on the troublous times we have briefly gone over in the foregoing pages, it is surprising what an amount of literature has come down to our times from a people so harassed and distressed.

We have already seen that the canon of Scripture was closed very shortly after the days of Nehemiah. The voice of inspiration had ceased, nor was it again heard till the "dayspring from on high" had visited His people (Luke 1:78), and God then spake to us in His Son. All later books than that of Malachi, the last of the prophets, have therefore no place in the Old Testament. But every book found in it has been authenticated by our Lord Himself when He declared "the Law, the Prophets and the Psalms" to be in very truth the word of God, and all included in "the Scripture which cannot be broken." The three divisions referred to above comprise all the books we call the Old Testament. They were held sacred and divinely inspired by the Jews, and no others were by them ever added. It was the Roman Catholic Council of Trent that first had the temerity to include the Apocrypha among the books reputed to be God-breathed. What the nature of this collection is we shall notice shortly.

It is necessary to be clear and positive as to the inspiration of the Old Testament, for efforts are not wanting in this unbelieving generation to shake the faith of the simple in books like Esther, Daniel, Jonah and others. But all of these were written ere the voice of prophecy was suspended; all the books now in our Bibles, and none other, were in the Bible loved, quoted and honored by the apostles, and endorsed as divinely-given by the Lord Jesus. He expressly refers to "Daniel the prophet," and "the sign of the prophet Jonah," in language that admits of no doubt as to the high plane on which He placed their writings.

But in the Maccabean age and later there were other books of instructive character, making no claim of inspiration, which the Jews have always valued, and which the early Christians sometimes read in their meetings for the sake of the lessons they contained, though with no thought of putting them on a level with the Hebrew Scriptures or the Greek New Testament.

These are the books collected by no one knows whom, and for convenience's sake designated *Apocrypha*—that is, "Hidden." Some of them are of finest literary quality; others are very inferior. Some, like 1 Maccabees, have distinct historical value; others are thoroughly unreliable and contradictory of known facts. All were written in Greek in the days of the great literary awakening which took place when Grecian culture was almost idolized by many of the Jews. The first book of the Apocrypha is known as:

I. Esdras, which is the Greek form of Ezra. This is largely a copy of the book of that name in our Bibles, with considerable added matter of very doubtful quality. The book was evidently produced in order to impress the educated Gentiles with God's care over the despised Jew.

THE GOLDEN CANDLESTICK FROM TITUS'S ARCH AT
ROME

II. Esdras is of an altogether different character, and
undoubtedly by a different hand. It is a book of strongly
apocalyptic style, consisting chiefly of a series of rapt
visions with more or less spirituality interwoven. The
writer evidently took Daniel, Ezekiel and Zechariah as
his models, and was one whose soul was inflamed by their
glorious promises of blessing coming upon Israel, and
fearful denunciations of judgment upon the foes of the
chosen people. On the other hand, it abounds with
inaccuracies and statements contradictory to the word of
God.

The book of **Tobit** professes to be a record of the
strange experiences of an Israelite of that name, who
belonged to the tribe of Naphtali, and was among those
carried away by the Assyrians. It is thoroughly unreliable;
a religious romance, full of absurdities, and yet teaching
lessons of morality and true piety. It is in this book that

we find an angel called Raphael. The only two angels actually named in Scripture are Michael and Gabriel. The incantations and thaumaturgic wonders of Tobit make it unworthy of the least credit, but add to its interest as an entertaining literary work. It, no doubt, often took the place in a Jewish home of many of the nursery tales of our own day, inculcating strict, moral and religious principles, with enough admixture of the marvellous to hold the attention of youth.

Judith is the story of the deliverance of Israel in the days of Nebuchadnezzar, by a Jewish matron, who goes alone into the camp of the enemy, gives herself into the power of the heathen general, Holofernes, for his destruction. When he becomes completely enamored of her wisdom and beauty, she takes him at an advantage and, while he sleeps, with his own sword she smites off his head. Whether there be any truth in the story or not, it is now impossible to say; but Judith has ever since been regarded as a national heroine, and her conduct viewed as on a very exalted level. Yet she deceives Holofernes, and does not hesitate to do evil that good may come; though preserving her own body inviolate.

With the exception of 1 Maccabees, the book of Judith is the finest narrative-work of the Apocrypha.

The omission of the name of God in the canonical book of Esther, caused it long to be questioned by the devout, who did not understand the divine reason for this. Hence we have in

"The rest of the chapters of the book of **Esther**, which are found neither in the Hebrew nor in the Chaldee," an effort to correct this. But it is a blundering attempt by a blundering scribe to improve God's perfect work. One only needs to read the inspired book of Esther, and then this marred human document, to observe the difference between God-breathed Scriptures and this human imitation.[5]

The next two books in the Apocrypha are to be classed in an altogether different category. They are among the finest specimens of uninspired wisdom literature, and are worthy of being ranked with the Discourses of Epictetus, the Morals of Marcus Aurelius, and the Essays of Bacon, though they are greatly inferior to the inspired book of Proverbs.

The Wisdom of Solomon is an anonymous work to which the great king's name is attached in the title. It is not of quite so high an order as the book that follows it, but is nevertheless of great value. The companion record is called:

"The Wisdom of Jesus the Son of Sirach, or **Ecclesiasticus**." It is generally conceded that this choice collection of proverbs and wise sayings is, as it professes to be, the production of Jesus (the Greek form of *Joshua*) the son of Sirach, who lived in the land "almost after all the prophets," and who has here embodied the sound instruction he received as a youth from his grandfather Jesus, who wrote in Hebrew, and died, "leaving this book almost perfected." The grandson translated, edited, and arranged it, making no claim to inspiration; he sent it forth hoping thereby to edify his nation, confessing his

---

[5] I have a little book called "Notes on Esther," which might help any who have never noticed the reasons for the omission of the divine name. Price, cloth, 50cts«, paper, 25 cts. Same publishers.

liability to error, but craving an unbiased reading of the work he had prepared in Greek from the Hebrew records left by the elder Jesus. The date given is in the years of Ptolemy Euergetes; and the praise of Simon the Just, in chapter 50, shows that the writer lived during his pontificate.

It will be remembered by Bible students that Jeremiah had a servant named Baruch. He it is who is presumed to be the author of the book of **Baruch**, the next in order. But there is no evidence that such was really the case. It is a work of little worth. The last chapter (6) professes to be "The Epistle of Jeremiah," written to the captives who were about to be led away to Babylon by Nebuchadnezzar. It is of a much less elevated order than the authentic writings of "the Weeping Prophet."

There are three tales which were added to the book of Daniel, and are given in order in the next section of the Apocrypha. The first is entitled:

"The Song of the Three Holy Children," and was added after the 23rd verse of Daniel, chap. 3. It pretends to give the song that the three Hebrew young men sang as they walked unhurt in the fiery furnace, and is of value as preserving the character of Jewish piety in the days we have been considering.

The History of Susanna was published as a preface to the canonical prophecy of Daniel. Shylock's exclamation, "A Daniel come to judgment!" upon listening to Portia's wisdom, finds its explanation here. It tells the story of the attempt of two lecherous elders, first to rob a young Jewish wife of her virtue, and upon being repulsed successfully, to blackmail the object of their vile but defeated purpose. Daniel, a mere youth, appears upon the scene, and by examining each of the villains separately, causes them to contradict one another in such a way as to establish both the innocence of Susanna and their own wickedness.

The third tale was added at the end of Daniel, and is called, "The History of the Destruction of **Bel and the Dragon.**" It is a wonder-tale, akin to that of Tobit, telling of a test made by Daniel and the Babylonians as to the power of the god Bel, and a great dragon who was overcome by Daniel through a mixture of pitch, fat and hair, which he thrust into the creature's mouth. One cannot fail to see in the whole foolish story the influence of Chaldean superstition as to charms and magical preparations on the mind of the writer. The miracles of the Bible are always of a serious, sober character, serving an important or useful purpose. They are never mere works of power, startling and bewildering with no moral motive. It is otherwise with the counterfeited signs of Satan's emissaries and with the wonder-works told in uninspired legends, such as that related in this un-historic history of "Bel and the Dragon."

The Prayer of Manasses purports to be the contrite supplication of Manasseh, the son of Hezekiah, upon his repentance. It is wholly fanciful, but interesting as giving an insight into Jewish piety.

I. Maccabees is a historical record of the wars of the Jews from the death of Alexander the Great to the pontificate of Simon the brother of Judas Maccabeus. It is from this book that our knowledge of the Jewish wars of independence has been mostly drawn. The style is vigorous and intensely dramatic, carrying the reader from scene to scene with unabated interest. As a testimony to the unfailing care of Jehovah for His people even when under His hand because of their sins, and His ready grace meeting them the moment they confess their iniquities and seek His face, the book is of great value. Yet the history makes no claim to divine inspiration. Who the author is, it is now impossible to say; but he was evidently a sincere lover of Israel and Israel's God.

II. Maccabees is much less reliable, though of great interest. It is a strange commingling of sober history and untrustworthy legend. The book is valued by the Roman church because of its apparent endorsement of the unscriptural custom of offering prayers for the dead. In chap. 12:43–45, Judas Maccabeus is said to have offered a sin-offering for the dead, and made thereby a reconciliation for them that they might be delivered from sin. Whatever may have been in the mind of Judas, his act has no Scriptural sanction.

There are two other books known as 3rd and 4th Maccabees, which were not included in the received Apocrypha by the Council of Trent, though it is declared by some that they were omitted by mistake. The first is fragmentary and legendary; the second, a lengthy, religious novel.

Other literary remains there are which were long valued by the Jews, but are now seldom read, and some completely lost; as, for instance, the Book of Enoch; the Secrets of Enoch; the Book of Jubilees; Testaments of the Twelve Patriarchs; Psalms of Solomon; Sibylline Oracles; Assumption of Moses; the Apocalypse of Elijah; the Apocalypse of Zephaniah, and some others, of which early Christian Fathers make mention, but which are no longer extant, so far as is now known. Some of these were begun during the days of the Asmoneans, and only completed in the Christian era; thus partaking of a mixed Jewish and Christian coloring. The Sibylline Oracles and the Book of Enoch are of this character.

It is a significant fact that in all the long years of the four silent centuries we have had before us, not so much as a psalm or any other literary product has come down to us that is worthy to be compared with the precious treasures of the Old Testament. Some, it is true, have attempted to assign Maccabean dates to some of the books of the Prophets and to several of the more recent psalms, but their guess-work theories are of no real value, and there can be little doubt that all were written when the last line of Malachi had been penned. The canon of the Jewish Scriptures was then complete. No desultory fragments were to be added in after years. When again the prophetic voice should be heard, it would be to announce the coming of Him who was the object and theme of "all the Scriptures," and whose advent in grace would be the occasion for the production of a New Testament completing the written revelation of God to man. The two volumes are the work of the one Spirit whose delight it was to "take of the things of Christ and show them unto us."

It is interesting and, from an educational standpoint, profitable, to familiarize oneself with these strange and ancient volumes; but all are as darkness itself when contrasted with the clear light that shines from the Sacred Oracles, the Holy Scriptures, given by inspiration of God for the furnishing of the man of God unto all good works; of which it is written,

"Forever, O Lord,
Thy Word is settled in heaven."

Made in the USA
Las Vegas, NV
06 February 2023

67012739R00062